Your Happy Healthy Pet™

Golden Retriever

2nd Edition

GET MORE!
Visit www.wiley.com/
go/goldenretriever

Peggy Moran

Howell
Book House™

Howell Book House

Published by Wiley Publishing, Inc., Hoboken, New Jersey

For general information on our other products and services or to obtain technical support please contact our Customer Care Department within the U.S. at (800) 762-2974, outside the U.S. at (317) 572-3993 or fax (317) 572-4002.

Wiley also publishes its books in a variety of electronic formats. Some content that appears in print may not be available in electronic books. For more information about Wiley products, please visit our web site at www.wiley.com.

Library of Congress Cataloging-in-Publication Data:

Moran, Peggy, date.
  Golden retriever / Peggy Moran. — 2nd ed.
    p. cm. — (Your happy healthy pet)
  Includes index.
  ISBN 978-0-470-19569-7
  1. Golden retriever. I. Title.
  SF429.G63M66 2008
  636.752'7—dc22
                                    2008001584

Printed in the United States of America

10 9 8 7 6 5 4 3 2 1

Book design by Melissa Auciello-Brogan
Cover design by Michael J. Freeland
Illustrations in chapter 9 by Shelley Norris and Karl Brandt
Book production by Wiley Publishing, Inc. Composition Services

About the Author

Peggy Moran has been working professionally to educate dogs and their owners since 1975. Her background includes training animal-shelter personnel, serving as the behavioral consultant to the American Dog Owners' Association, speaking at veterinary conferences, and guest lecturing about dog behavior at schools and universities.

Peggy was a monthly columnist, online editor, and feature writer for *DogWorld* from 1983 to 2002. She received the ASPCA's Pet Overpopulation Answers Award in 1999, through the Dog Writers Association of America, and has been featured on television and radio programs for her work with dogs.

Peggy lives with her husband, Dave; children Monica, Stephanie, and Jake; and many happy, healthy pets. She currently conducts classes at her Lemont, Illinois, training facility where she is assisted by her own two Golden Retrievers, Rowdy and Buddie.

About Howell Book House

Since 1961, Howell Book House has been America's premier publisher of pet books. We're dedicated to companion animals and the people who love them, and our books reflect that commitment. Our stable of authors—training experts, veterinarians, breeders, and other authorities—is second to none. And we've won more Maxwell Awards from the Dog Writers Association of America than any other publisher.

As we head toward the half-century mark, we're more committed than ever to providing new and innovative books, along with the classics our readers have grown to love. From bringing home a new puppy to competing in advanced equestrian events, Howell has the titles that keep animal lovers coming back again and again.

Contents

Shopping List

You'll need to do a bit of stocking up before you bring your new dog or puppy home. Below is a basic list of some must-have supplies. For more detailed information on the selection of each item below, consult chapter 5. For specific guidance on what grooming tools you'll need, review chapter 7.

☐ Food dish   ☐ Nail clippers

☐ Water dish   ☐ Chew toys

☐ Dog food   ☐ Play Toys

☐ Leash   ☐ Crate

☐ Collar   ☐ ID tag for collar

☐ Grooming tools (pin brush, slicker brush, bristle brush, two-sided comb, round-tip scissors, grooming spray, dog toothbrush and toothpaste, dog shampoo and conditioner, cotton makeup removal pads)

There are likely to be a few other items that you're dying to pick up before bringing your dog home. Use the following blanks to note any additional items you'll be shopping for.

☐ _____

☐ _____

☐ _____

☐ _____

☐ _____

☐ _____

☐ _____

☐ _____

☐ _____

☐ _____

☐ _____

Pet Sitter's Guide

We can be reached at (___)_____-_____ Cell phone (___)_____-_____

_____

We will return on _____ (date) at _____ (approximate time)

Dog's Name _____

Breed, Age, and Sex _____

Important Names and Numbers

Vet's Name _____ Phone (___)_____- _____

Address_____

Emergency Vet's Name _____ Phone (___)_____- _____

Address_____

Poison Control _____ (or call vet first)

Other individual to contact in case of emergency (someone the dog knows well and will respond to) or in case the dog is being protective and will not allow the pet sitter in _____

_____

Care Instructions

In the following three blanks let the sitter know what to feed, how much, and when; when the dog should go out; when to give treats; and when to exercise the dog.

Morning_____

_____

Afternoon_____

_____

Evening _____

_____

Medications needed (dosage and schedule) _____

_____

Any special medical conditions _____

_____

Grooming instructions _____

_____

My dog's favorite playtime activities, quirks, and other tips_____

_____

_____

Part I
The World of the Golden Retriever

The Golden Retriever

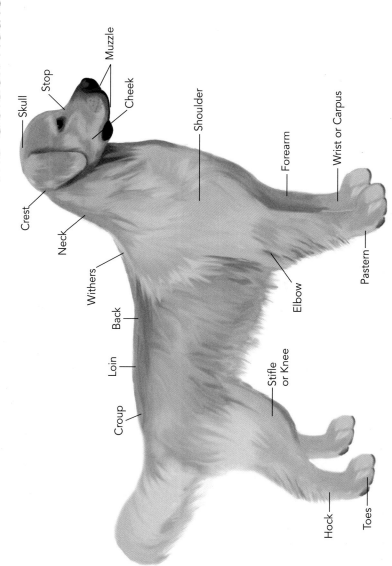

- Skull
- Stop
- Muzzle
- Cheek
- Crest
- Neck
- Withers
- Back
- Loin
- Croup
- Shoulder
- Forearm
- Wrist or Carpus
- Elbow
- Pastern
- Stifle or Knee
- Hock
- Toes

Chapter 1

What Is a Golden Retriever?

The Golden Retriever is a sporting dog with a kind, enthusiastic nature. Equally suited to both city and country lifestyles, the Golden is the perfect breed choice for active families of all sorts. Goldens are tolerant, sensitive, intelligent, and playful. Known for their patience as well as their enthusiasm, and bred to work in close cooperation with people, Goldens make wonderful companions for just about anyone. And anyone who has known or loved a Golden Retriever will tell you they are a dog to seek, keep, and treasure.

The Golden Retriever isn't just an awesome social companion; he is a capable sporting dog who excels in the field, a popular winner in the conformation ring, an enthusiastic obedience and performance competitor, and a devoted assistance dog to owners with special needs. A Golden Retriever may never have more of a job than to be a family pet, but he brings all of these wonderful potentials and abilities into his relationships with every person he meets.

Because of his kind temperament, the Golden Retriever is a trustworthy friend. Whether you are seeking the first best friend for your children or the ideal companion to put the gold in your golden years, this retriever can and will do it with grace and consideration.

Highly sensitive to social cues, Goldens really care about your feelings. Your Golden will pay attention to you, respond to your moods, and reflect his sensitivity every moment you are together. When you're feeling happy and enthusiastic, he'll be bouncing right along with you. During down times, there is nothing finer than the feeling of your loyal Golden turning to and reassuring you. You will never feel lonely when he is near.

The Golden Standard

Just about everyone has a mental picture of the Golden Retriever. Although you may have noticed differences in appearance between various Goldens, and probably even find these differences endearing, there really is an objectively "ideal" Golden Retriever.

The ideal Golden Retriever in the United States is described by the breed's official American Kennel Club breed standard, which was most recently revised in 1982. Many people think the standard only matters when looking at dogs from a snooty or show ring perspective; but upon closer examination, you'll probably agree the breed standard actually is of great importance to *all* Golden Retrievers. The standard is the guide breeders refer to when they are planning matings of dogs, with their goal being to produce the most structurally correct and healthy dogs as possible that are true to type. Because they have a standard to breed to, we can recognize an adult Golden and also confidently predict what our Golden puppy will look like when he grows up.

Variations from the standard can be very slight, such as a crooked tooth, or very extreme, such as when a dog has very crooked legs. Differences matter most when you intend to show and then breed your dog. If a structurally incorrect dog is bred, he may pass those faults and problem potentials to his offspring. Structural faults aren't just about breeding; they also can indicate an underlying tendency toward unsoundness that can result in poor health. If your otherwise healthy pet Golden Retriever seems less than ideal according to the breed standard's description, remember that he may not be of perfect breeding quality, but he is still *your* ideal, and that matters most of all!

The Golden Retriever is a sporting dog, and that heritage definitely influences his appearance and his behavior.

The Sum of All Parts

The emphasis when identifying the ideal Golden Retriever is on his overall appearance, personality, and working attitude and ability. The breed standard does offer a rather detailed breakdown of Golden Retriever individual parts, describing how they should look and fit together. If you are intent

What Is a Breed Standard?

A breed standard is a detailed description of the perfect dog of that breed. Breeders use the standard as a guide in their breeding programs, and judges use it to evaluate the dogs in conformation shows. The standard is written by the national breed club, using guidelines established by the registry that recognizes the breed (such as the AKC or UKC).

The first section of the breed standard gives a brief overview of the breed's history. Then it describes the dog's general appearance and size as an adult. Next is a detailed description of the head and neck, then the back and body, and the front and rear legs. The standard then describes the ideal coat and how the dog should be presented in the show ring. It also lists all acceptable colors, patterns, and markings. Then there's a section on how the dog moves, called *gait*. Finally, there's a general description of the dog's temperament.

Each section also lists characteristics that are considered to be faults or disqualifications in the conformation ring. Superficial faults in appearance are often what distinguish a pet-quality dog from a show- or competition-quality dog. However, some faults affect the way a dog moves or his overall health. And faults in temperament are serious business.

You can read all the AKC breed standards at www.akc.org.

on getting a show-quality Golden Retriever, study the breed standard and then attend dog shows to see which Goldens are the ones who are winning. The best breeders have an eye for puppies who have the potential to become champions.

If you are certain you want to show your Golden, be sure to tell your breeder well before you are at the point of selecting your puppy. She will help you all the way through the process. If you are just looking for a great Golden friend, you will get a pet-quality puppy. But don't worry that you are getting second quality. Sometimes developing dogs make little adjustments away from physical perfection; they can still be a great Golden Retriever and to an untrained eye will be just as lovely.

What does matter to anyone getting a Golden, and must never be accepted at a substandard level, is temperament. An aggressive or shy Golden puppy is substandard and should be avoided. Starting out with his best paw forward, your friendly, inquisitive, playful Golden will only improve with time and your loving attention.

Gold Medal Athletes

The ideal Golden Retriever is built for action. A sporting dog needs the correct structure for maximum athleticism so he can perform his job properly in the field. Even if your dog's sole purpose is to be a friend and companion, correct structure will help ensure an active life and great health. The strength and power described in the breed standard as "strong neck, broad front, straight legs, and correct angles" are required for a dog who might spend the day hunting and carrying birds through ground cover. These same qualities will guarantee him maximum athleticism while playing and spending active time with you in his everyday life.

General Appearance

Goldens look happy; they seem to nearly always have the dog equivalent of a smile on their face. The ideal Golden has a kindly expression and is eager, alert, and self-confident. He is symmetrical, powerful, and active, built for action—hunting—and shouldn't be clumsy or overly long-legged. Goldens in conformation shows are measured against the breed standard, but how well a dog is put together, how he moves, his fitness, and his attitude are all given more consideration than any of his individual features.

Beauty in Motion

Is there anything more beautiful to behold than a Golden Retriever in action? When trotting, his gait is free, smooth, powerful, and well coordinated, showing good reach. Viewed from any position, his legs turn neither in nor out, and his feet do not cross or interfere with each other while he is moving. A dog with proper structure will move correctly, and his fitness will improve through exercise, whereas a dog with poor structure may tire more easily and become sore or lame when exercising.

A Golden with proper structure will move elegantly and effortlessly.

Size

The ideal Golden is a midsize dog. Males measure 23 to 24 inches tall at the *withers* (the top point of the shoulder); females are 21½ to 22½ inches. Dogs who deviate more than 1 inch in height from the standard are disqualified in dog shows. The Golden should be slightly longer than he is tall.

The range for weight is 65 to 75 pounds for male Goldens and 55 to 65 pounds for females. The weight recommendations are meant for dogs of proper height who are in working condition. Obviously, an overweight dog or one suffering from poor nutrition will not fall within these weights. There is a tendency for Goldens to be larger (taller and heavier) than the standard allows, due to certain trends over the years, but an appropriately sized Golden is more suitable for the various jobs he performs and will be inclined toward better health.

All That Glitters

If there is one feature that truly defines the Golden Retriever, it is his coat and—most especially—his coat color: gold, of course! The variations observed in Golden Retriever coat color can cause confusion and lead us to ask the question: Just how gold *is* gold? Is reddish gold, or creamy, or nearly white gold still gold?

There are many possible shades of Golden gold.

According to the breed standard, a wide range of colors is permissible, from light to dark golden, and shade is really just a personal preference. Other than extremely pale or extremely dark, which are both considered undesirable, all the variations are allowed. Originally, most Goldens were darker gold, but during the last twenty years a lighter golden color has become more popular.

Feathering or *furnishings*—your dog's longer, flowing hair on his legs, body, and tail—may be lighter than the rest of the body. These light shadings are not to be confused with white markings. White markings anywhere on the body, other than a few white hairs on the chest, are considered a fault according to the breed standard. White markings anywhere on your Golden will not affect his quality as a loving companion or working dog, though, and the distinguished graying around the muzzle many aging Goldens develop is not penalized in the show ring.

Puppy Goldens are often lighter in their puppy coat than they will be once they shed and get their adult coat and color. A good way of guessing the adult color is to look at the darkest part of your puppy's ears; this is approximately what the adult body color will be.

Coat Quality

The Golden coat should act as a protection for this hunting breed, to protect him from the elements and the environment on land and in the water. Due to its length, a Golden's coat will pick up burrs and seeds that would never be found on a Labrador Retriever or Chesapeake Bay Retriever. Many hunters choose to trim their Golden's furnishings during hunting season, but on a properly coated pet Golden there shouldn't be much of a problem.

The Golden Retriever has a *top coat*—the hairs you see—that is dense and water-repellent. This outer coat, which lies close to the body, may be straight or wavy and should be neither coarse nor silky. Excessive length, *open coats*—where the hair stands out from the body and looks overly fluffy—and limp, soft coats are very undesirable.

Another visible part of your dog's coat is his feathering, which develops as he matures. The feathering is the Golden's crowning glory. Feathering is the moderately long, fringelike hair on the backs of his forelegs and on his underbody as well as on the front of his neck, the backs of his thighs, and the underside of his tail.

Your Golden also has a second coat you cannot see, called the undercoat. The *undercoat* is made of softer, lighter-colored hair that helps insulate your dog in all weather conditions. In the summer the Golden's coat helps keep environmental heat away from him, and in the winter it helps hold his body heat in.

The coat should repel water, rather than soak it up like a sponge. A Golden with a proper coat will come out of the water, shake a couple of times, and be nearly dry. The coat on your Golden's head, paws, and front of the legs is short and even. If the Golden coat is wavy, these waves are usually on the hair along the back. Occasionally you see a truly curly Golden, with curls all over his body while the hair on his legs, face, and feathers is straight. This is no doubt a throwback to the Tweed Water Spaniel that was used during the initial development of the breed (see chapter 2 for more on the history of the Golden).

That gorgeous coat should not be silky or fluffy. It was developed to protect a working dog.

Golden Retriever History

The Golden Retriever is a relatively recent breed, the product of deliberate breedings of other sporting dogs. Up until the early 1950s, a very colorful rumor circulated strongly implying that Golden Retrievers originally stemmed from a troupe of performing Russian Sheepdogs who had been purchased from a visiting circus while touring Britain. It turns out Goldens actually had their start in 1865, when sportsmen in Britain tried to produce a superior hunting dog.

Jolly Good Sports

The modern-day Golden Retriever's origin can be traced to the British Isles and a man named Sir Dudley Majoribanks, who later became the first Lord Tweedmouth. Lord Tweedmouth lived near Inverness, Scotland, during the 1800s, and, like many of the British gentry, he was involved in breeding sporting dogs. At the time, hunting methods and weapons were changing, and many birds could be shot and gathered during one outing. Lord Tweedmouth sought to breed a dog who possessed both a high drive to retrieve multiple birds as well as an excellent sense of smell for sniffing out wounded birds who had fallen into brush or water. The dog also had to have what is known as a soft mouth—the ability to retrieve birds in her mouth without biting down and crushing them.

Retrievers were considered the elite of the sporting dog breeds because they were so versatile and could be used for both waterfowl and upland game (other birds hunted for food). There were many crosses of breeds used during this time, no doubt including several Golden-like retrievers. But, unlike his peers who were also breeding sporting dogs, Lord Tweedmouth kept a Studbook (detailed records of all of his breedings) between 1835 and 1890. In 1952, his descendants made these breeding records available, allowing us to look into the earliest breed history of the Golden Retriever.

Lord Tweedmouth bought a male puppy he named Nous from a Brighton cobbler who'd been given the dog as payment on a debt. Nous was the only yellow puppy from an otherwise all-black litter of unregistered Wavy-Coated (now known as Flat-Coated) Retrievers. Although the Flat-Coated Retriever is primarily black, the recessive yellow color does occasionally occur and is referred to as a *sport*. Existing photos of Nous show a large, wavy-coated dog who looked very much like a modern Golden Retriever. Nous came to live at Lord Tweedmouth's residence, known as Guisachan, where he reportedly demonstrated enthusiastic hunting abilities.

Lord Tweedmouth next acquired a female Tweed Water Spaniel he named Belle. Now extinct, the Tweed Water Spaniel was another popular hunting breed of the time and region. Tweed Water Spaniels looked similar to the Irish Water Spaniel but with heavier muzzles and more pointed skulls. Tweed Water Spaniels, named for the Tweed River area where they were developed, were known for their swimming ability, superior intelligence, and wonderful temperament. The Tweed Water Spaniel is said to have contributed approximately a quarter of the Golden's genetic base, and most likely a great deal of the breed's inherent love of the water.

Mothers and Fathers of the Breed

Lord Tweedmouth's first breeding of Belle and Nous resulted in four yellow female puppies: Ada, Crocus, Cowslip, and Primrose. He kept Cowslip for his planned breedings, but her sisters also produced puppies who helped contribute to the development of the Golden Retriever as we know her today. In his efforts to add other desirable traits to his bloodlines, Lord Tweedmouth introduced two black Wavy-Coat Retrievers, a Red (Irish) Setter, and even a Bloodhound to the gene pool.

During this time, there were other sportsmen who had obtained dogs from Lord Tweedmouth and no doubt bred Golden-type dogs. However, none kept detailed records to document a formal breeding program.

The first Goldens were registered by the Kennel Club in Great Britain in 1903 and were listed as Wavy or Flat Coats Golden. The public became aware of the breed in 1908, when Lord Harcourt brought a collection of the dogs

Golden Retrievers were developed to retrieve waterfowl; they needed to be smart and trainable, good water dogs, and not bite down on the ducks in their mouth.

descended from Lord Tweedmouth's original breedings to the Kennel Club Dog Show. Lord Harcourt was a huge fan. He not only helped generate early breed awareness but is also credited with naming the breed.

Another important early fancier was Winifred Charlesworth, who became one of the breed's greatest enthusiasts. She acquired her first Golden in 1910 and proceeded to promote the breed as a true dual-purpose dog (excelling in both hunting and dog shows) until her death in 1954. Charlesworth's efforts resulted in the formation of the Golden Retriever Club of England in 1911, as well as the first breed standard, and, in 1913, registration with the Kennel Club as a separate breed. Charlesworth was the owner of many important Goldens, including Noranby Campfire, the first Golden Retriever to become a champion.

Getting to the USA

Goldens could be found in the United States as early as the 1890s; however, the breed did not make its official entry until the 1920s. This was an era when Americans were enamored of anything British, including their sporting dogs. Along with Labrador Retrievers, a few Goldens were imported by some of America's wealthiest and most prominent citizens. During World War II, some breeders sent their dogs to the United States for safety, adding more foundation dogs to the American Golden gene pool.

There are reports of Goldens throughout Canada and the United States in the early 1900s, but none of them were ever registered as Goldens. During these early years, Goldens were registered and shown as a type of Labrador Retriever.

Golden Retrievers didn't actually gain recognition as a separate American breed until 1932. During this time, as the handful of fanciers grew, some dogs were shown sporadically, and there was an occasional litter of Golden puppies. The first truly serious Golden breeder in the United States was Charles Large of New York City. Beginning in 1931, he imported a number of dogs who were shown and became the foundation of his breeding program. Large was an early activist in the attempt to form a national breed club, but his efforts were never realized because he died in 1933. Luckily, his dogs were acquired by another man who continued Large's breeding program.

The Golden Retriever finally received the boost it needed when Colonel Samuel Magoffin of Vancouver, British Columbia, imported a young male from England named Speedwell Pluto in 1932. Pluto was a champion in both the United States and Canada. He was the first Golden to win a Best in Show award and was a successful hunting dog as well. He is considered to be the foundation sire of the breed in America.

Magoffin imported a number of dogs from Britain who would become influential in the development of the breed. He had kennels in Vancouver and Colorado and had relatives in Minnesota and Wisconsin who also imported

It's only relatively recently that Goldens have been thought of as anything other than hunting dogs.

What Is the AKC?

The American Kennel Club (AKC) is the oldest and largest pure-bred dog registry in the United States. Its main function is to record the pedigrees of dogs of the breeds it recognizes. While AKC registration papers are a guarantee that a dog is pure-bred, they are absolutely not a guarantee of the quality of the dog—as the AKC itself will tell you.

The AKC makes the rules for all the canine sporting events it sanctions and approves judges for those events. It is also involved in various public education programs and legislative efforts regarding dog ownership. More recently, the AKC has helped establish a foundation to study canine health issues and a program to register microchip numbers for companion-animal owners. The AKC has no individual members—its members are national and local breed clubs and clubs dedicated to various competitive sports.

Goldens. The dogs they bred were some of the most influential producers as the breed developed in the late 1940s and 1950s, and were successful in both conformation shows and field trials.

Striking Gold in America

Through the mid-1940s, half of the Golden litters registered by the American Kennel Club were whelped in southeastern Minnesota. This was an era when hunting upland game and waterfowl was enjoying a peak in popularity among a growing number of hunters, and the Midwest was the capital of this pastime. The Golden was embraced by many hunters as the dog for the job. Midwestern fanciers helped form the Golden Retriever Club of America in 1939.

Following World War II, a growing number of Americans now had the money and leisure time to include a dog in the family, yet the Golden was still relatively unknown to the general public as a pet. Most were in the hands of show and field competitors or hunters. It was rare to find a Golden in the average home.

That changed in 1974, when a young female named Liberty found her way into the White House as President Gerald Ford's pet. When Liberty produced "first puppies," the Golden Retriever became an overnight sensation. Registrations skyrocketed, and Goldens quickly rose to become one of the AKC's top five most popular breeds—where they have remained ever since.

Many Goldens and their breeders have been instrumental in shaping the breed as we know it today. A more detailed look at the "who's who" of both foundation breeders and their dogs is an important next step for anyone hoping to become more involved in breeding, showing, or just really knowing about Goldens. The box on page 24 lists some of these early achievers.

The All-Purpose Golden

Though once primarily sought after for her abilities as a hunting dog, the Golden also has a more recent history as a helper in a variety of jobs. Goldens have worked as service dogs to people with disabilities, guides for the blind, and helping ears for the deaf. Goldens have been trained and used as rescue dogs in numerous situations, such as after earthquakes and avalanches and seeking lost persons. Their natural scenting abilities, along with the ability to concentrate on the task at hand, made and continue to make them popular dogs for such work.

Since the 1970s, the Golden's popularity as a pet has soared. Their versatility and easygoing attitude make them great family dogs.

Early Golden Achievers

In the field: *Field trials* are hunting tests that offer sporting-dog breeders, trainers, and owners the opportunity to prove their dogs' competency in the field and earn titles. The first Golden to place in a British field trial was reported in 1904. A Golden Retriever was entered in the first AKC-Licensed Retriever Field Trial held on Long Island in 1931. The first American Field Champion was awarded to FC Rip in 1939.

In the conformation (show) ring: At conformation shows, dogs are judged on how well they conform to the breed standard. Championships are awarded to dogs who win a specific number of points from several different judges. Dogs who are champions are considered of superior breeding quality because they have been objectively measured for qualities that will enhance the breed or hold true to breed type. In 1908, Culham Brass and Culham Copper were the first Goldens to place first in dog shows in Britain. In 1932, Am/Can Ch. Speedwell Pluto became the first American Golden Retriever champion, and in 1933 he was the first Golden to win a Best in Show.

In the obedience ring: *Obedience trials* provide competitive challenges where dogs and their handlers work together to prove their training and cooperation and earn titles. The first GRCA National Obedience Trial was held in 1950, where Ch. Gunner of Featherquest won the first High in Trial award. When the American Kennel Club first offered Obedience Trial Championships (OTCH) titles in the early 1970s, Golden Retrievers were the first three recipients. Since then, more Goldens have earned the title than any other breed. Goldens from all backgrounds can excel in obedience; it just takes a willing attitude and a kind trainer.

The ideal Golden is equally at home in a hunting blind and a show ring.

Goldens have been loved with a devotion Lord Tweedmouth and others in the breed's early history would be proud to see. Unfortunately, there is a concern that the modern Golden breed has split into two, three, or even more distinct types with different purposes.

Not very long ago, Goldens who were successful in different activities often came from the same litter. Dogs whose primary purpose was to work with a hunter could also be shown, and many show champions were not only good field dogs but produced good working dogs as well. While there were extremes at either end, the breed for the most part was considered dual-purpose. Now, many field dogs no longer resemble Golden Retrievers. The same can be said for many dogs bred strictly for showing in the conformation ring, whose heavy bone structure and excessive coat make them unfit to be working dogs.

Serious breeders strive to produce a Golden who fits the standard in all ways and can be used for whatever purposes his owner desires, whether that's hunting, obedience, sport, the show ring, assistance, or companionship. The people who helped make today's Golden produced a hunting dog and a steadfast companion of very specific structure and type. Anyone who breeds their Golden must be certain their dog's puppies will be the best Golden Retrievers possible, in every way. Only dogs of superior health, temperament, conformation, and working ability should contribute to the Golden Retriever gene pool, and not every dog, no matter how great she is as a pet, is of breeding quality. As the Golden you know and love steps out of history and into your heart and life, it is important to remember her earlier admirers' intentions and plans.

Chapter 3

Why Choose a Golden?

Golden Retrievers have so many attractive qualities that it's hard to imagine why you wouldn't choose one. With their tolerant temperament, sweet face, athletic body, gorgeous coat, willing work ethic, and high trainability, they are easy dogs to love. Whether you were first attracted to their looks, kindness, intelligence, or abilities, you probably appreciate Goldens for all these attributes. When looking for a Golden Retriever as a pet, most people hope for a dog who expresses every desirable aspect of the breed, and most Goldens not only live up to these expectations, they exceed them.

Although Goldens all share many qualities, keep in mind that no two dogs—not even siblings—will be exactly the same. Personalities differ from one dog to the next, and those differences help us make a unique and special bond with one specific dog. The descriptions in this chapter will help you understand the breed in general, but each Golden you are lucky enough to meet will introduce you to his own subtle spin on being a Golden Retriever.

The Social Golden

Joyful and outgoing, Goldens naturally make friends and gain fans wherever they go. When walking a Golden, don't be surprised if you make your own new friendships with people who share your appreciation for this popular breed. Goldens are often the favorite clients of veterinarians, dog groomers, and obedience instructors.

They are usually the teacher's pet at dog training school. Goldens learn easily when shown what is desired of them and do not ever require harsh corrections.

Though resilient and not easily offended, punishment and strong disapproval will hurt their feelings and confidence. When they do experience an upset, though, they are quick to bounce back as soon as the situation is remedied.

It is this resiliency and adaptability that makes the Golden Retriever ideal for so many different purposes. The confident, cooperative Golden can safely guide the blind, competently assist the deaf, and empathically provide therapy to elderly or infirm people. Working and service dogs have to be able to enter any situation or environment and stay on task despite distractions. Adaptability makes placing a rescued Golden who

The adaptable Golden makes an excellent service dog.

needs a new home easier than it is for some other breeds. While he may initially miss his former home and owner, it probably won't show; he will quickly transfer his love to new people who treat him in a loving way.

Not Watchdogs

Unlike some breeds, which tend to form one-person or single-family attachments, the Golden shares his affections freely with many. Though he will form an especially strong bond with the people who care for, train, or spend the most time with him, it will never be to the exclusion of others.

Typically, Goldens don't make the best guard dogs. They are generally not excessive barkers, though they will alert their owners to unusual incidents such as strange sounds or intruders. While dogs of other breeds might bark, growl at, and even threaten a stranger, a Golden may bark in excitement—unless he already has something in his mouth.

They Crave Affection

Goldens crave affection and can be pushy in their pursuit of it. Without the right early education and appropriate responses from people who help teach proper behavior, a Golden can become overbearing. If a dog is successful in demanding attention from people who were otherwise occupied, he will become

These are extremely social dogs. They crave petting and affection.

more and more insistent. While at first it might seem cute and even flattering that he loves you so much, when he is repeatedly shoving his nose under your hand or arm, you may regret having been the one to be trained.

The Golden loves petting and will sit and soak it up for hours. He will want to get as close as he can, climbing right into your lap if you allow him, unaware he is mighty big for a lap dog. Being very orally oriented, he may try to give you a big, slobbery dog kiss, which you may or may not appreciate. The key to not creating a rude Golden Retriever is to reinforce him with calm, quiet attention when the timing is right for you as well as for him.

Trainability and Intelligence

Goldens are one of the most trainable breeds of dog. When a Golden seems stubborn, uncooperative, or slow, there is probably either an underlying trust issue or a lack of the right sort of training. With patient, positive reinforcement, he'll be giving you his best in no time.

Positive-reinforcement training methods focus on showing a dog what to do and rewarding him at just the right time and with great enthusiasm, rather than focus on what he should not do. Food treats can be useful motivators, but so can play, petting, freedom—anything he values. It is important to help him learn to cooperate in pursuit of life's rewards as part of a team, rather than to be forced or bribed to perform rote tricks. Goldens can be easily distracted by the smells, sights, and sounds around them, but can also learn that access to those interesting things is best achieved with your help.

When I talk about intelligence in dogs, I am referring to the ability to solve problems and quickly learn tasks. Golden Retrievers are intelligent dogs, but people sometimes see them as more sweet and beautiful than brainy. The distracted, unmotivated dog is probably not lacking intelligence, but lacking the right kind

The Dog's Senses

The dog's eyes are designed so that he can see well in relative darkness, has excellent peripheral vision, and is very good at tracking moving objects—all skills that are important to a carnivore. Dogs also have good depth perception. Those advantages come at a price, though: Dogs are nearsighted and are slow to change the focus of their vision. It's a myth that dogs are color-blind. However, while they can see some (but not all) colors, their eyes were designed to most clearly perceive subtle shades of gray—an advantage when they are hunting in low light.

Dogs have about six times fewer taste buds on their tongue than humans do. They can taste sweet, sour, bitter, and salty tastes, but with so few taste buds it's likely that their sense of taste is not very refined.

A dog's ears can swivel independently, like radar dishes, to pick up sounds and pinpoint their location. Dogs can locate a sound in $\frac{6}{100}$ of a second and hear sound four times farther away than we can (which is why there is no reason to yell at your dog). They can also hear sounds at far higher pitches than we can.

In their first few days of life, puppies primarily use their sense of touch to navigate their world. Whiskers on the face, above the eyes and below the jaws are sensitive enough to detect changes in airflow. Dogs also have touch-sensitive nerve endings all over their bodies, including on their paws.

Smell may be a dog's most remarkable sense. Dogs have about 220 million scent receptors in their nose, compared to about 5 million in humans, and a large part of the canine brain is devoted to interpreting scent. Not only can dogs smell scents that are very faint, but they can also accurately distinguish between those scents. In other words, when you smell a pot of spaghetti sauce cooking, your dog probably smells tomatoes and onions and garlic and oregano and whatever else is in the pot.

Goldens are extremely trainable. They just need the right motivation and positive reinforcement.

of training. A Golden may know exactly what is wanted and how to do it, but refuses because he lacks motivation. Some would blame the dog, calling him stubborn, but the truth is that it is up to his people to find a way to make cooperation pleasing *to the dog*.

Natural Instincts

One of the main reasons hunters have sought Goldens over the years is for their superior scenting ability. The instinct and desire to use their noses to discover and enjoy new and old smells is ever-present in Goldens. On walks or just in their yard, they are constantly on the alert for good scents.

The *retriever* part of the breed's name tells you the type of work for which they were developed. It is also an indication that the average Golden with natural instincts is going to spend a good deal of time looking for and carrying in his mouth any objects he finds. Anything within reach and not nailed down may be "retrieved": toys, books, shoes, dishtowels, socks, the cat, dirty underwear—all are likely targets for a retriever's mouth. Goldens are known for their gentle, "soft" mouths, but along the way tooth marks may appear on many of the items they retrieve.

However, Goldens can become mouthy, play-biting dogs unless they are appropriately discouraged. The dog who gently reaches up and grabs the forearm of his well-trained humans and then leads them on a tour of the house or to the door for a Golden-motivated walk may be cute, but is behaving inappropriately. Allowing this sort of manipulation can lead to other inappropriate behaviors. The teething puppy has no legitimate reason to teethe on human limbs, so be sure not to indulge mouthing behavior.

Golden Temperament

The temperament of a dog is determined by hereditary traits that are shaped by his environment and experience, especially during the first 22 weeks of life. Puppies go through a series of critical periods of development during this time, and it is important to be certain they are properly socialized. Any scary or traumatic events, or even the lack of social experience, can prevent a pup from developing into the dog he was genetically meant to be.

Sporting dogs are bred to work for long periods at a time and often have a higher level of energy than many other breeds. This energy is usually easily controlled, and a normal Golden should calm down quickly. A Golden who is ignored, given little exercise, and secluded from attention can develop an overexcitable personality resulting in stress and disruptive behavior.

While the Golden is known far and wide for his sweet, tolerant personality, unfortunately, there are aggressive exceptions. Aggressive dogs pose a risk to others and to themselves—a dog who causes harm will not last long in his home. Aggression can be learned, it can be caused by a health disorder, or it can be the result of bad breeding. It is very important not to breed dogs just because they live nearby or have registration papers. The science of breeding is complex and should be left to professionals who know how to keep the breed strong and true to type.

Certain behaviors should never be tolerated in a Golden. Aggressive actions toward humans, such as growling, snapping, or biting, are totally out of character with the breed. It is too easy to try to explain the actions of the Golden who bites a hand when removing a food dish or removing something from his mouth as "protecting what is his." But this is not acceptable behavior from any dog. Shyness and spookiness are also not in character with the temperament of the Golden. A dog who hides at the sight of visitors or tries to run from anything new may make a satisfactory pet with patience and work, but he should never be bred because such traits are usually genetic.

Golden Retrievers were bred to carry things in their mouth. This is a natural instinct that some dogs may take too far.

Goldens may chase cats, so peaceful coexistence is not always possible.

Regarding Other Creatures

Although you may think of your dog as a person in dog packaging, your Golden really is a *dog*. And being a dog, he will exhibit doggy traits. Generally, Goldens get along well with other domesticated animals. While it is not a desirable trait, adult males can be aggressive toward other dogs of the same sex. Occasionally, females will exhibit the same tendency. Neutering can help control this problem.

Goldens with a strong prey instinct will chase anything that runs from them, such as cats and rabbits—anything small and fast. They are more likely to bark at larger animals than chase them, though you can never be certain.

Of particular interest to Goldens are birds. For those dogs who come from strong hunting or field backgrounds, this bird interest could be called an obsession. If you keep chickens or ducks, or if you have a pet bird, it may be unrealistic for a Golden and birds to coexist without some form of physical separation.

Children and Goldens seem to be a natural pair, and usually they are. Some Goldens can be intimidated by boisterous youngsters, though, while others take just about anything in stride. It isn't a good idea to allow children to spend unsupervised time with any dog until you are certain everyone will behave appropriately. Some Goldens are too active, or too possessive of objects, to be trusted with children. The child may be accidentally injured when she is knocked down or playfully grabbed at. Likewise, a child can hurt a young puppy by rough play. All young children need to be supervised with any pet—all times.

Chapter 4

Choosing Your Golden

By now you are certain the Golden Retriever is the breed for you, and you're ready to start looking for your perfect dog. Researching your choice of breed means you are being careful and thoughtful about the whole process, rather than rushing into it. As you draw closer to the reality of getting your own Golden Retriever, the questions of where to get your Golden and which dog to select require careful consideration. Take your time and be patient! Getting the best dog from an appropriate source and being well prepared before you bring your new dog home will make the process easier on everyone. Whether you choose a puppy, an adolescent, or an adult; male or female; with a slightly lighter, darker, or wavier coat, the dog you choose will have all the traits that make the Golden Retriever perfect.

The Best Breeder

Your perfect dog starts with a perfect breeder. The best place to get a puppy Golden is from a reputable breeder who has experience participating in competitive events such as dog shows, obedience competitions, and field trials. These are places where objective judges can help breeders decide whether the dogs they are showing are truly sound enough to breed. Only the best all-around Goldens should contribute to the breed's gene pool.

The reputable breeder will be a participating member of his local and national breed club, and will be proud of that fact. He will not be satisfied with his dogs' beauty, type, and working ability alone. His dogs will have exemplary

Reputable breeders belong to breed clubs and compete in canine sports to prove the soundness of their bloodlines.

temperaments and documented physical soundness. He will know all about the ancestry of his dogs, to be certain they come from long lines of ideal Golden Retrievers. He will know a great deal about genetics and the process of selecting dogs who will complement one another, and the breed, when paired. His goal is to breed puppies who all conform closely to every aspect of the Golden Retriever standard.

Dogs bred this way will also make wonderful pets. Dog shows and trials objectively prove a breeder's success. Beware the breeder who tells you he "doesn't believe in showing" and only "breeds for temperament." *Every* Golden should be bred for temperament, while also conforming to the breed standard.

The breeder you choose should be helpful, encouraging, and willing to spend time talking with you and answering your questions. He will want to know about your home, family, and lifestyle in order to help you select the right dog for you. He will also want to be certain you will be right for one of his babies and will give that dog the best possible home.

He will want to meet you and your family, and will want you to meet his dogs. He will show you their health certificates, pedigrees, and awards, and if the sire isn't at the premises, he will still have lots of information about the dog, as well as photos. Even if he has several dogs, he knows each one well. They are well groomed, friendly, and happy, and he has a loving relationship with each of them.

A reputable breeder doesn't breed more than one or two litters a year, and when you decide you want a puppy from him, you will be placed on a waiting list. A red flag is the breeder with an ad in the paper and puppies available *now.* Also beware the breeder with an array of breeds to shop from. The Golden breeder loves his breed and produces only a limited number of superior-quality puppies for suitable homes.

First Impressions

Finding the best breeders begins with networking. Contact the local breed club and ask for a list of member breeders. The Golden Retriever Club of America has a list of breeder-referral contacts at their Web site (www.grca.org), and that is another excellent place to start. If you already know a lovely, perfect Golden, ask her owner where she came from. Attending a dog show or obedience trial is a great way to start meeting wonderful Goldens and knowledgeable breeders. You'll get to see which breeders have dogs who impress you—and the judges!

When you find an interesting breeder, your first contact will probably be by phone. During this initial conversation, there are a couple of important questions to ask. Obviously, an unfriendly breeder will be off-putting, but so should one who has lots of puppies available. Good breeders have waiting lists, and you should be prepared not to have immediate puppy gratification. Don't worry—your perfect Golden is worth the wait!

After the preliminary investigation, you will have narrowed your options down to a few top breeders. Next, you will want to pay each a visit to meet him and his dogs. When you arrive, expect to see and smell signs of cleanliness and order. Look for clean pens, clean runs, clean floors, and clean dogs. The adult dogs should be enjoying the run of the house and not be relegated to cages, the basement, or an outbuilding. They should greet you in a friendly, trusting way. All of your initial observations and first impressions should give you a feeling that says, "This breeder's puppies get a great start."

The Waiting Begins

Once you've found the best breeder and have discussed contracts, met dogs, made friends, and asked many questions, it will be time to be placed on a waiting list for the next litter. This usually requires a deposit paid up front. The price range varies depending on the breeder, his dogs, and the costs he has put into his breeding program. Expect to pay quite a bit more to purchase a purebred puppy than you would to adopt an adult dog.

You may decide to have a backup plan. There is always the risk a female may not conceive, or a litter may be too small, or the female may even have a health problem that results in puppies who are not suitable. If you are worried about winding up puppy-less after a long wait, and if you have found more than one perfect breeder, you might decide to put deposits on two prospective litters. If you do, be sure to inform both breeders and plan to give up your deposit on the backup puppy.

Now it's time to wait, plan, and get ready. Channel the time and your anticipation into lots of reading, learning, and preparing. This will benefit both you and your special new Golden when she finally comes home.

Meeting the Puppies

Although it seems like forever, in no time you'll get the announcement: The puppies are born! And then there will be still *more* waiting while they grow, develop, and learn about life. But soon enough the puppies will be ready for your first visit, and then at last it is time to meet them.

At the breeder's home the puppies will be kept in an area where they receive lots of attention and exposure to the sounds of an active household. Being in a calm but central area is very important to the puppies' future personalities and to their adaptability in their new homes. They may be located in the kitchen or in a spare bedroom, but not in a garage, a basement, or a remote outbuilding.

The puppies will probably be in a pen, and their pen will look and smell clean. It should be large enough that it can be divided in half: one side for potty and one for sleep and play.

The puppies will be solidly built, with strong bones, clean skin with no parasites or sores, have bright eyes with no discharge, and have clean ears with no odor. Their stools may be soft but will not be runny, and will be cleaned up quickly. They will have access to lots of fresh water and have toys to play with.

Mom-dog may or may not be present when you are introduced to her puppies. If she is, be sure to pay lots of attention to her first and praise the good job she has done. Next—and this will be hard—find a place to sit quietly and just observe the litter, rather than rush to pick up a puppy. By watching them interact with each other, their mother, their breeder, and finally you, you'll be able to learn a lot about each pup's individual personality. They may all look like little Golden peas in a pod, but they are each unique.

The breeder may have already selected a puppy who is just right for you. If so, trust his judgment. He knows his dogs and can help you get just the right one. If you do play a part in the selection process, try to make a decision based on suitability, not just "cute-ability."

The area where the puppies are kept should be clean and not in a place where the pups would be isolated.

You may have a gender preference, but it's good to know that both male and female Goldens are equally loving, intelligent, and trainable. Females can be a bit more independent, and males can seem to be the big teddy bears, but honestly, the differences are slight if they are there at all. Gender-specific concerns, such as *marking* (urinating to leave scent) and heat cycles, are easily neutralized by neutering your dog at the appropriate time. Both the breeder and your veterinarian will be able to advise you about neutering. The breeder may actually require neutering as part of his contract with you.

A Closer Look

Looking at the puppies, you may notice darker shading around their ears and faces. The ear-flap color of a puppy pretty accurately demonstrates what her adult body color will be. But remember, Goldens can have light undercoats and furnishings that may give their adult appearance a lighter overall effect.

Watching the pups (hopefully, not when they're napping), you may observe play fighting. All puppies do this, and it is their normal way of working out social status. When they aren't playing, the puppies will be showing interest in their mom, the breeder, and you. You'll notice some puppies are more excitable and active, and others seem more laidback. Keep in mind that high excitability can lead to rough and problematic behavior without proper training and supervision. The laidback dog is a cool character, but she can still be playful and rambunctious. None of the puppies should demonstrate flightiness, fear, or aggression toward each other or people.

Watch at feeding time and you'll discover if any puppies are extra pushy. This may appeal to you if you want a high-drive dog and you plan to do field work. But pushiness can translate into problems if younger children are going to be in the picture. The more passive, less competitive puppy will make an easygoing pet.

When you do get to hold and interact with the puppies, the breeder may hand them to you one at a time or allow you to just go right on in and interact freely with the group. When you are petting, does the puppy relax or become more intense? Does she lick or bite hard? If you are holding the *right* puppy, you will feel the beginnings of a deep connection being formed, and you'll just *know*—she is *the one.*

Your Adct Golden

Despite all of this puppy talk, perhaps you know the Golden bundle of fluff just isn't right for you. An adolescent or adult Golden might be a perfect fit. Each developmental stage has its pros and cons when it comes to bringing home your new Golden Retriever.

The young puppy is most adaptable because she is still forming her personality and will learn to think of your home and all of its social dynamics as normal. Because of the extreme sensitivity a puppy has to her surroundings in the first 22 weeks of life, she requires a large amount of time, training, and socialization. Her housetraining will require diligent supervision and frequent trips outside to

Look at each pup as an individual and also how they interact with the other pups. You'll begin to see which are more pushy and which are more laidback.

eliminate. During her teething stage, which begins at about 4.5 months, everything is at risk of being chewed up. The puppy herself is at risk from any hazard she happens to get her mouth on—electrical cords, toxins, poisonous plants. A young puppy requires a puppy-proofed house as well as a safe place for containment when she can't be carefully watched.

The adolescent Golden is ready to connect in a more developed and personal way, and is readily responsive to training. Provided she had a correct start somewhere else, the adolescent Golden can still bring lots of puppy fun but also a level of maturity the young puppy needs time to develop. Breeders sometimes keep a puppy for several months to see if she develops show potential. Sometimes a minor fault, such as slightly crooked teeth, rules her out as a breeding prospect but makes her perfect as a pet. The adolescent Golden who lived in the breeder's home has a handle on housetraining, manners, and socialization. Her adoption fee will be reasonable; the breeder really just wants proof she will be well cared for and have a loving, permanent home.

Some people think adoption is an easy way to get an inexpensive dog. It is true that adoption fees are generally very reasonable and often include neutering, vaccinations, and microchipping (a form of permanent identification). But there is no such thing as a free dog. Besides the adoption fee, there will be costs such as a veterinary exam, vaccinations, supplies, and equipment.

With an adult Golden, what you see is what you get. If the adult Golden comes from a breeder, she will probably be quick to adapt. So will the Golden who was raised in a foster home but then didn't work out as an assistance dog. Dogs given up by their owner are more risky, since adult dogs do not adapt and change as readily as puppies. What you might *not* see, at least at first, are behavioral and socialization problems she could be bringing with her from her past. Giving a needy adult Golden a home can provide you with a devoted loving friend who needs a second chance, but you do run the risk of also adopting someone else's mistakes.

Housetraining, socialization, and behavior problems are not uncommon with secondhand dogs. The dog with behavioral and social baggage may have trouble settling down and requires a loving, patient, and caring home. If you choose to adopt an adult Golden, especially through a rescue or adoption group, plan to work with a professional trainer or behaviorist. This will give you and your dog the best chance at a happy life together.

Golden Retriever Rescue Groups

Golden rescue groups consist of breed enthusiasts and caring animal lovers. These Golden guardians work hard to provide down-on-their-luck, homeless dogs with second chances at happy lives. Rescue groups scout local shelters for

An adolescent or young adult dog won't require the intensive supervision that a puppy needs.

Goldens, and when they find them, pull them out and put the dogs into foster care. Once in a foster home, the rescued Golden is assessed, vaccinated, neutered, microchipped, wormed, checked for heartworms, trained, groomed, loved . . . and then given up again—but only to a carefully qualified, *permanent* home.

Rescue groups are easy to find and will be thrilled to hear from you. You can visit the national breed club's Web site (www.grca.org) or inquire through local shelters, all-breed dog clubs, and breeders. Just get on the Internet and search for "Golden Retriever Rescue," and you'll be amazed by how many resources pop up.

When adopting a rescue dog, there will be a waiting process, even for dogs badly in need of homes. These dogs require carefully considered placement. To adopt a rescued Golden, you must fill out an application, provide referrals, and probably have a home inspection. During all of this, you will be gathering your own information about the dogs you are considering. Ask lots of questions. Why was this dog given up? Who did she live with? Was she around other pets? Is she good with children?

The people in the rescue group will appreciate your questions and do their best to provide answers. Your interest demonstrates dedication and promises you will provide one of their homeless Goldens with a wonderful "forever" home. The fee you pay will be reasonable, especially considering all of the costs and time they have already put into your dog. Be generous and pay above the required fee if you can afford it; you'll be helping to provide future rescued Goldens with the same loving care.

The puppy-fuzzy stage passes quickly, so enjoy it—and take lots of photos.

There are plenty of wonderful adult Goldens available for adoption.

Almost Home

Of course, you held out and are waiting to get your Golden from a reputable breeder or Golden rescue group. The breeder will not release your puppy before she is 7 weeks of age, and more likely not before 8 weeks. Many breeders will keep the puppies even longer, to be certain they have had the best start and their second set of shots at 12 weeks.

When the puppies are ready to go to their new homes, the breeder will prefer that their new families pick them up in person. The puppies will have had their first vaccinations and worming, and will have been examined by a veterinarian.

The adolescent and adult dog will ideally meet you several times before coming home, to give you time to get to know each other and be certain you are a good fit. Spend time alone together, walking and playing. Ask if you can feed the dog, to see if she becomes overly possessive of food. If you have another dog, be sure to bring her and introduce the two on neutral territory to make sure they will get along. If the adult Golden is in a shelter or rescue group, she will need to be neutered before being allowed to come home with you.

Whichever Golden Retriever you have chosen, plan to take lots of photos so you can remember the day your Golden finally comes home!

Part II

Caring for Your Golden Retriever

Chapter 5

Bringing Your Golden Home

While waiting for your new Golden Retriever, try channeling some of your excitement and anticipation into preparing for his arrival. Essentials you are going to need are listed on page 49. With this information, you can make a shopping list before heading off to the pet-supply store; it will help you avoid buying too many unnecessary items. Yes, it is fun to buy those cute bandanas, colorful collars, and adorable dog toys—but it's best to focus first on getting the things you'll really need to have on hand. Having everything ready before your Golden comes home will reduce stress for all involved.

Confinement

The first topic to consider is space. Where will your Golden be spending time? Will he have access to the entire house or will he be limited to certain rooms? It will be simpler to housetrain your puppy if he is confined to specific areas when you aren't directly supervising him.

Crate, Sweet Crate

One of the most important pieces of equipment to obtain before your Golden comes home is a crate. The crate is a small denlike space (like a very little room) where your dog can be safely kept when nobody is available to supervise him. In nature, wild dogs den in small caves when they are biding their time and resting.

The crate will protect your dog from hurting himself and also help prevent indoor accidents during his alone times. The crate will actually help increase your Golden's early security in your home. Using the crate correctly won't make you your new Golden's jailer; just be sure to provide him with safe chewing materials and never leave him in the crate for very long. Crating should not be for longer than two hours with younger puppies and no more than six hours with mature adults.

There are two types of crates. Metal wire ones offer good visibility and air circulation, while plastic airline-type crates are best for travel in cars and for keeping dogs in bedrooms. The plastic crate will contain shed hair and is somewhat

Safe confinement will keep your puppy out of trouble.

quieter than metal ones, but can also be isolating and overly warm. Some people decide to invest in both types and keep the wire crate in a main area of the house and the plastic crate where the dog will sleep.

Whichever sort you get, be sure the crate is large enough to accommodate a full-grown Golden. A crate that will fit an adult Golden is approximately twenty-four inches wide, thirty-six inches deep, and twenty-six inches high. Floor space can be reduced by dividing the crate with a wire panel (sold with better-quality wire crates); otherwise, your puppy may mistake one side for an indoor toilet. The subdivided crate must provide enough space for your Golden to comfortably stand, turn around, and lie down.

When you are home, leave the crate open and toss some toys in it to help your Golden to get comfortable coming and going. When you do close the door, it will be less stressful because he doesn't associate the crate only with confinement. Bedding may help your Golden develop a taste for fabric shredding as a form of self-entertainment. If your dog swallows large amounts of fabric, he can develop a life-threatening intestinal blockage. Generally, dogs will seek cooler resting areas, so don't feel bad about the bare crate tray. If you do decide to provide bedding, make sure it is something that can't easily be shred or ingested and that can be washed repeatedly.

Baby Gates and Exercise Pens

Gates can be used to keep your puppy enclosed in areas with easily washed floors, allowing him some freedom with easy cleanup. Even if you have an interior door you could close, it is better to leave it open and use a baby gate instead. Closed doors create more frustration than gates, which allow visibility.

However, gates can be dangerous. The wooden, accordion-folding type have large spaces puppies can get their heads stuck in. Pressure-mounted wooden slatted gates are better, but may tempt teething Golden puppies to chew on the rails. The plastic gates that have sturdy, close-woven mesh are the best. Climbing over a gate can be dangerous for you and your puppy. Get the type you can swing open and closed.

The exercise pen is a set of panels that open up to form a small yard. The two ends clip together with bolt snaps, creating an open-topped containment for safe puppy play. Never leave your Golden untended in the pen; it is not inescapable, and many dogs quickly figure out how to get either over or under the panels.

Tying Out vs. Tethering

Never tie your Golden outside and leave him. Dogs who are tied out can hurt themselves or become tangled. Your pet doesn't need to be left alone outside for hours; he is a social companion who would prefer to be with you.

Never tie your dog out alone in the yard. When your dog is outside, he still wants to be with you.

Tethering your dog indoors—to a person but *never* a stationary object—is a mobile confinement method and a great way to spend lots of time with your Golden. When he is attached to you, you'll have no worries about what he might be up to in the next room. Keeping him near you by tying his leash around your waist and then going about your daily routine will *really* help you build a bond with your dog!

Fun Stuff!

Golden Retrievers are playful, interactive, and *love* to retrieve. On land, in the water, anywhere the toy goes, your Golden will follow, and most will return the toy to you. Don't be discouraged if your dog isn't an immediate retriever-achiever. With a bit of training, encouragement, and time, he will be retrieving like a champ.

Your Golden will be inclined to chew in response to boredom and stress, so you'll want to have lots of fun chewing stuff around. A Kong is an oddly shaped, hollow, rubber toy you can stuff with peanut butter or a tasty treat. The Kong will keep your Golden occupied for hours. It is totally washable and can be scrubbed on the inside with a bottle brush to make sure the stuffing doesn't spoil.

Pet-safe rubber balls are great fun, and so are the splash balls made for children to soak and throw at each other. They are lightweight and washable and provide a big, soft mouthful of toy—something Goldens really enjoy. Fleecy stuffed toys (often shaped like a gingerbread boy) are also pleasing to the discriminating retriever mouth.

Floating water toys, if you are lucky enough to live near a safe swimming area, can be repeatedly retrieved without putting undue stress on developing bones and joints. You can buy floating retrieving dummies—canvas and rubber stuffed tubes—that are attached to a long, plastic rope and can be tossed out into the water and pulled back in again to help build your dog's interest without having to get your feet wet. If you are willing to go into the water, your Golden is very sure to follow and figure out the whole swimming thing very quickly.

> **TIP**
>
> If you take your dog swimming, be sure it is in clean water, that your dog can walk in and out, is supervised by you, and knows how to dog paddle.

Toys to Avoid

Soft plastic toys and toys with squeakers inside can wind up chewed apart and swallowed, and may lead to dangerous intestinal blockage. If you must see your

Toys aren't just for puppies. Your Golden will enjoy them all his life.

Golden walking around with big goofy dentures, a fake hotdog, or a rubber pork chop, please do not leave him untended with those items—ever.

Two-sided tugging toys are fine as long as you teach your Golden to play respectfully and let go on command.

It isn't a good idea to give your Golden socks or old shoes to play with; his interest may easily broaden to any sock and any shoe. Most Goldens are more likely to collect, hoard, and cuddle your possessions than to all-out destroy them, but these objects are still likely to end up with tooth marks and holes.

Outdoor Puppy-Proofing

The box on pages 52–53 explains how to protect both your home and your puppy. Once you've taken care of puppy-proofing the house, it's time to take a look around your yard. Check every bit of fencing to be sure there are no loose boards or wire, and be sure there are no low spots where your Golden might try to crawl or squeeze under. Protect your gardens and flower beds with wire fencing, or he may start digging up bouquets and bulbs and delivering them to you, full of pride and lots of extra cultivated soil. A marking sound (explained in chapter 9) such as "eht!" along with a loud clap, is usually enough to nip Golden gardening behavior in the bud.

Puppy Essentials

You'll need to go shopping *before* you bring your puppy home. There are many, many adorable and tempting items at pet-supply stores, but these are the basics.

- **Food and water dishes.** Look for bowls that are wide and low or weighted in the bottom so they will be harder to tip over. Stainless steel bowls are a good choice because they are easy to clean (plastic never gets completely clean) and almost impossible to break. Avoid bowls that place the food and water side by side in one unit—it's too easy for your dog to get his water dirty that way.
- **Leash.** A six-foot leather leash will be easy on your hands and very strong.
- **Collar.** Start with a nylon buckle collar. For a perfect fit, you should be able to insert two fingers between the collar and your pup's neck. Your dog will need larger collars as he grows up.
- **Crate.** Choose a sturdy crate that is easy to clean and large enough for your puppy to stand up, turn around, and lie down in.
- **Nail cutters.** Get a good, sharp pair that are the appropriate size for the nails you will be cutting. Your dog's breeder or veterinarian can give you some guidance here.
- **Grooming tools.** Different kinds of dogs need different kinds of grooming tools. See chapter 7 for advice on what to buy.
- **Chew toys.** Dogs *must* chew, especially puppies. Make sure you get things that won't break or crumble off in little bits, which the dog can choke on. Very hard plastic bones are a good choice. Dogs love rawhide bones, too, but pieces of the rawhide can get caught in your dog's throat, so they should only be allowed when you are there to supervise.
- **Toys.** Watch for sharp edges and unsafe items such as plastic eyes that can be swallowed. Many toys come with squeakers, which dogs can also tear out and swallow. All dogs will eventually destroy their toys; as each toy is torn apart, replace it with a new one.

If your dog really digs digging, you can quickly deter him with a gross but effective trick: Bury some of his poop in the hole, cover it with a thin layer of the soil he loosened up for you, and then watch him change his mind the next time he visits his *ex*-favorite digging spot.

The Big Day

Finally it is *the* day—the day you get to bring home your Golden Retriever! Arrange to pick him up in the morning so he has the whole day to adapt before he has to try to sleep in an unfamiliar place. Before you start on your journey home, try to get him to relieve himself, and if you have a long road trip, also plan to stop along the way at safe rest areas where you can give him the chance to eliminate. He may vomit from the ride and stress, but hopefully his meal was withheld before the trip to reduce this possibility. Be sure to bring cleaning wipes, paper towels, and a few small waste bags just in case.

For the ride home, you can break the rule of always having your Golden ride in a secured, plastic crate (or, as he gets older, a seatbelt harness) and let him ride home cuddled in a blanket on a passenger's lap. This is a crucial bonding moment; he may be a bit upset, and your comforting attention will be appreciated. Speaking of attention, plan not to have a houseful of guests waiting to be the puppy's welcoming committee. Also make sure your family members—especially children—understand he needs to be greeted calmly and then allowed some space and quiet time to settle in.

Remove poisonous plants from your garden to keep your dog safe.

Welcome Home!

When you arrive home, take your beautiful new Golden straight to his designated potty area. Next, encourage him to follow you into the house and allow him to check things out. It's a good time for him to learn to navigate between his indoor and outdoor areas, so resist the urge to carry him. He may be hesitant at first, but if you squat down, clap your hands a bit, and say "here, puppy, puppy" in an encouraging voice, he will probably make his way right to you. Puppies will follow instinctively, especially if they are feeling unsure.

Once he moves toward you, keep retreating toward the gated-off area you have prepared for him. If he pauses along the way to check everything out, let him. He is meeting his new home for the very first time, and all the smells need to be sorted out.

When you've made your way to his gated area, allow your Golden to walk around and investigate at his own pace. During all of this initial exploration he may pause and pee. If he does, don't make a fuss—just clean it up (and read chapter 10!). Blot up his first accident with paper towels and then bring them outside and weigh them down with a rock in his designated toilet area. The scent of the pee-infused towels will help

inspire him to make more—outside, where you want him to. Cleaning up accidents with an enzyme-based cleaning product will address the same issue—scent attraction—from the opposite angle. The enzymes in the cleaner will destroy the bacteria that creates the scent dogs are attracted to.

Good Night

You and your family can sit on the kitchen floor and speak sweetly to your Golden puppy, but don't pick him up or pester him while he is trying to get his bearings. His open crate, some toys, and a bowl of water should all be located in easy reach within his area, and the area shouldn't be too far from the door he'll be using to go outside. You can position a cuddle bed or blanket on the floor outside the crate, which will provide a nice resting spot—for both of you. Your Golden puppy will need to nap frequently and soundly throughout the day. Be sure everyone understands how important rest is to growing puppies; he must never be disturbed or awakened from naps or he may become anxious or even cranky.

When bedtime rolls around, he may be too exhausted to care, but it is best to anticipate that he may feel lonely and displaced. Some people sleep downstairs near their puppies for the first few nights, and others use the second-crate-in-the-bedroom approach and have their puppy sleep near them. The in-room approach seems to reduce excitability and is especially important if the dog will have to spend longer stretches of time alone during the day.

Puppy-Proofing Your Home

You can prevent much of the destruction puppies can cause and keep your new dog safe by looking at your home and yard from a dog's point of view. Get down on all fours and look around. Do you see loose electrical wires, cords dangling from the blinds, or chewy shoes on the floor? Your pup will see them too!

In the kitchen:

- Put all knives and other utensils away in drawers.
- Get a trash can with a tight-fitting lid.
- Put all household cleaners in cupboards that close securely; consider using childproof latches on the cabinet doors.

In the bathroom:

- Keep all household cleaners, medicines, vitamins, shampoos, bath products, perfumes, makeup, nail polish remover, and other personal products in cupboards that close securely; consider using childproof latches on the cabinet doors.
- Get a trash can with a tight-fitting lid.
- Don't use toilet bowl cleaners that release chemicals into the bowl every time you flush.
- Keep the toilet bowl lid down.
- Throw away potpourri and any solid air fresheners.

In the bedroom:

- Securely put away all potentially dangerous items, including medicines and medicine containers, vitamins and supplements, perfumes, and makeup.
- Put all your jewelry, barrettes, and hairpins in secure boxes.
- Pick up all socks, shoes, and other chewables.

In the rest of the house:

- Tape up or cover electrical cords; consider childproof covers for unused outlets.
- Knot or tie up any dangling cords from curtains, blinds, and the telephone.

- Securely put away all potentially dangerous items, including medicines and medicine containers, vitamins and supplements, cigarettes, cigars, pipes and pipe tobacco, pens, pencils, felt-tip markers, craft and sewing supplies, and laundry products.
- Put all houseplants out of reach.
- Move breakable items off low tables and shelves.
- Pick up all chewable items, including television and electronics remote controls, cell phones, shoes, socks, slippers and sandals, food, dishes, cups and utensils, toys, books and magazines, and anything else that can be chewed on.

In the garage:

- Store all gardening supplies and pool chemicals out of reach of the dog.
- Store all antifreeze, oil, and other car fluids securely, and clean up any spills by hosing them down for at least ten minutes.
- Put all dangerous substances on high shelves or in cupboards that close securely; consider using childproof latches on the cabinet doors.
- Pick up and put away all tools.
- Sweep the floor for nails and other small, sharp items.

In the yard:

- Put the gardening tools away after each use.
- Make sure the kids put away their toys when they're finished playing.
- Keep the pool covered or otherwise restrict your pup's access to it when you're not there to supervise.
- Secure the cords on backyard lights and other appliances.
- Inspect your fence thoroughly. If there are any gaps or holes in the fence, fix them.
- Make sure you have no toxic plants in the garden.

Puppies must chew. Hard nylon bones are a safe chew toy.

The thought may cross your mind to have your Golden sleep right in bed with you, but give careful consideration to the big picture—the big dog picture, that is. An adult Golden is going to be a significant bedmate, and sleeping with you can lead to some misperceptions regarding just whose bed it is. This can be especially problematic when there are babies or small children who could be hurt if they climbed into your bed along with the very large dog, or if the dog jumped into your bed and landed on them. If you decide to have your Golden in bed with you (you'll never be cold again), be sure he has a designated spot at the foot of the bed and is only allowed up by invitation. And don't start the practice until he can get through the night without a potty break.

Into the Mouths of Babes . . .

. . . *Everything* will go! As your puppy goes from shy, new baby to family member, you will notice he is about 40 percent mouth. The mouth is a dog's grasping tool, and everything of interest goes into it. Some things shouldn't go there, and some never come back out.

Swallowing inedible materials poses a life-threatening risk of bowel obstruction. Anything you give to your dog must therefore be large enough that it cannot be swallowed. Providing your Golden with interesting, safe chewing items will reduce wear and tear on your possessions and protect your dog. It is best to give a puppy a few choice toys rather than too many. The more things a puppy has, the more difficulty he'll have differentiating what belongs to him and what does not.

Stuffed Kong toys, mentioned earlier, are great for chewing and so are both nylon and heavy (unbreakable) sterilized shank bones. These are not bones left over from your dinner; they are pet-safe natural bones sold at the pet-supply store. Rawhide chews should be given with caution. Some dogs are overzealous in trying to swallow the chewed pieces, and if they're large enough, these pieces can get lodged in the throat. When swallowed, they produce a lot of gas.

Quality Time

Before your Golden Retriever comes home, you'll think a lot about all the time you'll soon be spending together. But when the actual day arrives, you may be surprised to discover just how much time your puppy actually requires. People who work full time and have very busy lives should think twice about getting any dog, but especially a young, impressionable, energetic puppy. The thought of a lonely Golden puppy ticking away long hours conjures a sad picture. Dogs left home alone all day become terribly overexcited and rambunctious when people are present. Your puppy will need someone at home to help him develop social skills and confidence, and for potty training.

If you do work and still intend to have a dog, make sure you can locate and afford to pay a pet sitter to come over midday to let him out and provide attention and care. Adult dogs may better tolerate being left alone, but it still isn't very natural or humane. Wild dogs live in dynamic groups with ongoing social and physical interaction.

Most Goldens reach their peak of activity and need the least amount of rest from 6 months to 3 years of age. As they mature, they spend increasingly longer periods of time sleeping. It's important to make sure your Golden gets enough exercise each day to keep him fit and at the right weight throughout his life. Puppies need short periods of low-impact exercise to protect them from injury. Walks are great, but if they're longer than a mile, plan to take several rest periods along the way. Adult dogs can go farther, but make sure you always bring water and that the weather is not too hot.

While adult Goldens are flexible and adaptable, puppies do best when they stick to a schedule.

Chapter 6

Feeding Your Golden Retriever

Your Golden Retriever's health and life expectancy are maximized by good genetics, responsible care, and excellent nutrition. You have a major role in keeping your Golden well by making the best choices for her nutrition. As your Golden matures and her activity levels change, so will her nutritional needs. A proper diet that includes the right nutrients in balanced amounts and proportions with free access to fresh water will help keep your Golden healthy and happy.

The best place to start researching the right diet for your Golden is with her breeder. The breeder has already done all her homework and will be able to tell you exactly what and how much to feed your dog. The food your puppy has been eating at the breeder's place is what you should feed her at home, at least at first.

If you do decide to change dog foods, never do it all at once because your puppy will develop an upset stomach. Her little gut isn't made for variety. Introduce a food change gradually, replacing small quantities of the old food with equally small portions of the new, and gradually build toward a total switch.

Dogs do not need to have daily or weekly flavor changes. In fact, their appetites are motivated by smell more than taste. Goldens are not finicky eaters, so no worries about a nose being turned up—they will eat just about *anything*.

The Golden's healthy, "eat anything" appetite can actually get her into trouble. A Golden will eat whatever smells good, and way more of it than she needs. As a result, Goldens can easily become overweight. Obsessive food drive usually results in socially unbecoming (rude!) behaviors, such as begging, scavenging, and stealing.

Commercial versus Natural Food

With concerns about commercial pet food safety and a growing desire to care for pets in the most natural ways possible, many pet owners decide to feed their Goldens homemade meals rather than commercial dog foods. Feeding a homemade diet should only be done with the aid of books on canine nutrition or the guidance of a veterinary nutritionist.

An adolescent dog requires a much higher intake of protein, calories, and nutrients than an adult dog, due to the demands of her rapidly developing body. Most commercial brands of dry kibble meet these requirements and are well balanced for proper growth. Commercial dog foods are well researched by huge companies that spend millions of dollars to prove their products are nutritious and appropriate for the average dog.

A big problem in recent pet care history actually stems from pet owners caring too much. People tend to overfeed, and especially oversupplement, their dogs in hopes of guaranteeing them perfect health. But instead, too many dogs suffer from obesity and other diet-related problems. Feeding growing Golden puppies foods that promote soft-tissue development and make them bulk up before they have completed their skeletal growth puts undue stress on joints. High protein levels and high fat intake are suspected of contributing to panosteitis, a painful inflammatory disease of growing dogs' long bones.

Water is as important a part of your dog's diet as all the other nutrients.

Dry or Canned?

Dry, kibbled food has some advantages over canned foods. It's less expensive than canned food of equal quality. Wet foods stick to teeth and contribute to tooth decay, calcium deposits, and gum disease. Canned foods also have high water content, meaning the actual amount of nutrient your dog is getting may be less than it would appear. Canned foods also smell, and they spoil soon after the can is opened.

Canned foods do offer some advantages, though. Due to the higher percentage of meat-based products and higher water content, they can be useful to stimulate appetites and are easy to digest. As a supplement to dry dog food, canned foods can also help with needed weight gain.

Nutritious Ingredients

When you are reading the ingredients list on a bag of food, meat should have top billing. That's because ingredients are listed in descending order based on quantity. Meat provides your Golden with essential protein and improves food palatability and digestibility. Protein requirements vary from 15 percent for older dogs to 26 or even 28 percent for puppies (I'm talking here about dry food). Food with 21 to 23 percent protein is suitable for the average adult Golden. It is best to avoid super-high protein levels unless your Golden is a super athlete; otherwise, there will be undue stress placed on the dog's excretory organs.

You can share your food with your dog, but choose the food carefully and don't overdo it.

Reading Dog Food Labels

Dog food labels are not always easy to read, but if you know what to look for they can tell you a lot about what your dog is eating.

- The label should have a statement saying the dog food meets or exceeds the American Association of Feed Control Officials (AAFCO) nutritional guidelines. If the dog food doesn't meet AAFCO guidelines, it can't be considered complete and balanced, and can cause nutritional deficiencies.
- The guaranteed analysis lists the minimum percentages of crude protein and crude fat and the maximum percentages of crude fiber and water. AAFCO requires a minimum of 18 percent crude protein for adult dogs and 22 percent crude protein for puppies on a dry matter basis (that means with the water removed; canned foods will have less protein because they have more water). Dog food must also have a minimum of 5 percent crude fat for adults and 8 percent crude fat for puppies.
- The ingredients list the most common item in the food first, and so on until you get to the least common item, which is listed last.
- Look for a dog food that lists an animal protein source first, such as chicken or poultry meat, and that has other protein sources listed among the top five ingredients. That's because a food that lists chicken, wheat, wheat gluten, corn, and wheat fiber as the first five ingredients has more chicken than wheat, but may not have more chicken than all the grain products put together.
- Other ingredients may include a digestible carbohydrate source (such as sweet potatoes or squash), fat, vitamins and minerals, preservatives, fiber, and sometimes other additives purported to be healthy.
- Some grocery store or generic brands may add artificial colors, sugar, and fillers—all of which should be avoided.

Working your way down the ingredient list on the bag of dog food, your next concern is grain content. Goldens tend to be allergy-prone, and grains such as wheat, soy, and corn won't help. Allergies usually manifest as skin problems or an inability to properly digest the food, and can be confirmed by veterinary tests. Grains such as ground brown rice, barley, and oats are better and tend to be well-tolerated by most Goldens.

Pet Food versus People Food

Many of the foods we eat are excellent sources of nutrients—after all, we do just fine on them. But dogs, just like us, need the right combination of meat and other ingredients for a complete and balanced diet, and simply giving the dog a bowl of meat doesn't provide that. In the wild, dogs eat the fur, skin, bones, and guts of their prey, and sometimes even the contents of the stomach.

This doesn't mean your dog can't eat what you eat. If your dog is eating a commercial dog food, you can still give her a little meat, dairy, bread, some fruits, or vegetables as a treat. Fresh foods have natural enzymes that processed foods don't have. Just remember, we're talking about the same food you eat, not the gristly, greasy leftovers you would normally toss in the trash. Stay away from sugar, too, and remember that chocolate is toxic to dogs.

If you want to share your food with your dog, be sure the total amount you give her each day doesn't make up more than 15 percent of her diet, and that the rest of what you feed her is a top-quality complete and balanced dog food. (More people food could upset the balance of nutrients in the commercial food.)

Can your dog eat an entirely homemade diet? Certainly, if you are willing to work at it. Any homemade diet will have to be carefully balanced, with all the right nutrients in just the right amounts. It requires a lot of research to make a proper homemade diet, but it can be done. It's best to work with a veterinary nutritionist.

Adding Meat and Vegetables

In reading about Goldens and talking about dogs with other dog lovers, you will inevitably hear mention of raw food or BARF diets. (*BARF* stands for bones and raw food.) This holistic approach to feeding looks at the way dogs in nature would eat and then tries to mimic it. If this is an approach to feeding you'd like to consider, be sure to discuss the pros and cons with your veterinarian and your dog's breeder and do lots of research first.

If you'd like to take a more moderate approach and still offer your dog some of nature's bounty, try supplementing her commercial diet with a small amount of meat and fresh vegetables. Raw meat poses some risk of bacterial contamination if it isn't eaten right away, but in small, quickly consumed quantities, it makes a fine supplement. And remember, feeding meat—raw or cooked—by itself won't provide your Golden with adequate nutrition.

Pureed vegetables—raw or cooked—can add some dietary interest without increasing total caloric intake too drastically. Dogs have trouble digesting the cellulose in whole raw vegetables but can easily handle them if they are pureed, and benefit from their natural vitamins and antioxidants. Since Goldens really like to chow down, it's important to feed them foods that won't pack on the pounds. Any vegetables will do, except onions, which contain substances that are toxic to dogs.

You can grind everything up—veggies and meat—and store the dog stew in a covered container in your refrigerator for several days. Add a tablespoon or two to her kibble at each meal and she will be a very happy, healthy Golden Retriever.

Feeding a Growing Golden

Your Golden puppy will need three meals a day until she is at least 4 months old. Offer three meals until she is 6 months old, but don't be surprised if she starts to walk away from a half-eaten lunch. Most puppies will naturally begin to wean themselves off a midday feeding, at which point you can simply divide the total amount she was being fed per day into two meals instead of three.

When you cut your puppy down to two meals, she will start to have an easier time with housetraining. Because she is eating less frequently, she'll produce more concentrated, less frequent bowel movements. You can't just leap to two meals with a younger puppy in hopes of accelerating potty training though. Your young Golden's tummy is too small to hold enough food to provide energy for all-day playing and growing.

Feed your Golden in an area where she can eat without interruption, but where she won't feel so isolated that she becomes too distressed to focus on her meal. Your kitchen or an adjacent utility room are both good options. If you have more than one dog, it's important to feed them separately or at least under direct supervision. Some people with several dogs feed them in their crates to prevent food fights and make sure every dog gets her fair share.

Puppy Teething

Don't be surprised if your 4-month-old Golden suddenly stops wanting to eat much, if any, of her food. This is when she begins to lose baby teeth and gain her adult ones, and it can be a period of great discomfort. Soaking her food to soften it and giving her frozen teething toys will help. Once she is over the teething, her appetite will resume. If it doesn't, it is important to visit the vet to see if your Golden has any other underlying medical problem contributing to her loss of appetite.

Examine your dog's mouth intermittently to be certain she isn't retaining any baby teeth alongside her new adult ones. Sometimes the baby teeth stay in and decay and infect the adult teeth. If this happens, your vet will remove the stubborn baby teeth.

Feed your dog someplace where she won't be isolated, but also won't be interrupted.

Set your puppy's food down at scheduled meal times and leave her with it for fifteen to thirty minutes. At the end of her meal, pick up her dish and store or throw away any leftovers. Some people start right out letting their puppies eat as much as they want at each meal and allow the dog to naturally regulate her appetite. If your Golden seems like a bottomless pit, this may not be the best plan. Rapid weight gain puts too much strain on a growing puppy's frame and entire system. You'll need to give her measured portions of food to prevent her from eating until she is sick, even if she is underweight.

Follow the instructions provided by your vet or breeder, not the dog-food bag, regarding quantity. The suggestions for portions on dog-food bags are general and are not always correct for a particular dog's food needs.

In the *very* unlikely event your Golden puppy loses her appetite, don't try to coax her into eating by hand feeding. If she has been eating

> **TIP**
>
> The ribs or bones of a puppy should never protrude or be visible. This is a sign that nutritional needs are not being met. Though not visible, when you place your hands on the body of the pup, those ribs should be easy to feel. If your hands sink into the body, cut back on food.

normally but suddenly stops, see your veterinarian. If she has just come into your home and lacks appetite, it may simply be stress. Fight the urge to start plying her with special treats and just keep presenting her normal meals at their scheduled times. She should start eating in almost no time. Of course, if she doesn't, consult your vet.

Keeping Adults in Good Weight

By 6 months of age you can eliminate the lunch meal and feed your Golden two meals per day. Providing your adult dog with scheduled meals helps you anticipate her bowel movements and prevents her from overeating. Some people feed their dogs just once a day, but dogs sometimes get hungry if fed only one meal a day. There is also some concern that one meal a day may contribute to bloat (see page 91 for more information).

The amount of food an adult Golden should eat daily will vary according to the size of the dog, her activity level, and how much time she spends outside. If all other factors are equal, a dog who spends a lot of time outside will require more food in colder months than warmer ones. A small, moderately active, female Golden who weighs about fifty pounds and lives in a mild climate may only need three cups of quality maintenance dog food per day. A large male under the same circumstances may consume five to six cups and stay in good weight. The extremely athletic Golden may need to eat a performance food with higher protein levels (28 percent) to maintain good health and high energy levels.

Thin Is In

Did you know dogs kept close to their safest lean weight actually have significantly increased life expectancy—as much as two years? As your Golden becomes an adult it may be a challenge to keep her at her perfect lean weight. Remember Goldens *love* to eat! It is up to you to protect her from her appetite. Lots of exercise and activities will help, but can't compensate for overfeeding. Hip dysplasia—a malformation of the hip socket and femoral head—hopefully won't be a problem for your Golden, but sadly, it is a genetic health problem that plagues the breed. Lean dogs have fewer problems with their hips than overweight, heavy-load-bearing ones—especially if the hips are dysplastic.

When your Golden is done growing from puppy to adult, her metabolism will slow down. She will not need to eat as much food, but won't appreciate a reduction in meal size. You can try feeding a healthy weight-reduction diet under your veterinarian's supervision if she really starts to pack on pounds despite your diligent control of her meals.

Weight gain can be a symptom of an underlying medical condition such as a thyroid problem. If you are concerned her weight gain is disproportionate to her food intake, talk to your vet. Be sure you know her entire food intake; check to see if family members are slipping her scraps and table food. Remind everyone that your Golden will live a longer, healthier life if they fight the urge to share their food.

If you feel she needs an occasional snack to tide her over, give her a natural bone or a Kong toy with a tiny amount of peanut butter smeared inside. The

Growing puppies need more nutrient-dense food and more frequent meals than adults require.

Keep your dog fit and active by keeping her in good weight.

licking and chewing she'll have to do to get those few calories will help her appetite feel sated without making her plump.

Golden Years: Fit, Not Fat

Even while she retains her puppy playfulness and youthful good looks, your Golden will gradually grow older, and her food needs will begin to change. When she reaches the age of about 8, it will be time to switch to a food that is lower in fat, unless she is still very active. Dogs do not need lower protein levels as they age unless they have kidney problems. In fact, there is some evidence that keeping up protein levels will prevent muscle wasting.

Maintaining the proper weight and nutrition of your older Golden is probably more difficult than at any other stage of life. A certain amount of body fat is necessary to protect her in the event of illness, but too much weight will make her even less active and more prone to physical problems. If an aging dog develops problems such as kidney failure, heart disease, or an overly sensitive digestive tract, there are specially formulated foods your veterinarian can provide. These prescription diets will meet the nutritional needs of a dog without further aggravating the physical problem.

The Golden who is fed quality food and kept at an optimum weight for her size will truly be a happy, healthy Golden Retriever all of her life.

Chapter 7

Grooming Your Golden Retriever

As a breed, Goldens require a minimum amount of regular grooming to remain clean and attractive. A little brushing, an occasional bath, and a bit of trimming pretty much cover the grooming needs of your Golden. Some people like to send their dog for professional grooming, which involves bathing, blow drying, conditioning, trimming the feathering, removing any *mats* (snarled clumps of hair that form behind ears, under forelimbs, and anywhere else, especially areas with soft, fine hair that tangles easily), nail trimming, and the finishing touch of a colorful bandana. While professional grooming isn't necessary, you may decide to indulge yourself and your dog now and then.

Grooming Equipment

Before going into the how-tos of keeping your Golden well groomed, you need to have the right equipment on hand.

Brushes

You'll want to have three types of brushes in your grooming kit. That's a lot, but each plays a different part in keeping your Golden looking gorgeous. The first is a pin brush, which looks like a small paddle with a raised rubber cushion with ball-tipped pins sticking out of it. The pin brush is used to remove dead hair and foreign substances from your Golden's coat.

Use a bristle brush to smooth your dog's topcoat.

The second brush to have is a slicker brush, which has a handle with a rectangular head that has many closely grouped rows of tiny metal wires that are all bent in the same direction. The slicker brush is used to remove shed hair and to smoothe your Golden's fine undercoat and feathering.

The third brush is a bristle brush. This brush looks like a good-quality, bristle brush for humans and is used last, to smoothe the topcoat and give it that distinctive Golden Retriever sheen.

Combs

A fine-tooth comb, often called a flea comb, removes dirt and—you guessed it—fleas. A two-sided comb, known as a cat comb (although it is for your dog), has widely spaced teeth on one end and close-together teeth on the other. Combs are used to pull small nasties out of your Golden's coat. It is important to check the tips of any comb you purchase to make sure they are rounded and won't scrape your Golden's skin.

Nail Clippers and Scissors

Human nail clippers can be used on puppies until they are about 3 months old. These make it easier to remove just the tips of tiny nails. Dog nail clippers come in two basic styles. One type has two blades and works like a pair of scissors. The other style has an oblong opening that the nail fits in and a single blade that cuts the nail when the movable handle is squeezed. Either works well. Besides large nail clippers, you should buy a commercially available styptic powder specifically for dog nails. Keep it on hand in case you cut a nail too short.

Medium-size scissors with rounded tips are used to trim the excess hair between your Golden's toes and also any extra-long feathering.

Grooming Spray

Grooming sprays keep hair damp while you are brushing it, helping prevent breakage and loosening tangles. They also condition coats, skin, and may even protect from sun damage if they have added sunscreen. There are many types of sprays to choose from, but those that contain tea-tree oil (*Melaleuca alternifolia*) offer the added benefit of being mildly repelling to mosquitoes, fleas, and ticks. Because Goldens are prone to skin sensitivities, you may decide to buy a spray made specifically for sensitive dogs.

A Golden Retriever is not a wash-and-wear dog. That long, flowing coat requires upkeep.

Shampoo and Conditioner

While it might be tempting to use your own shampoo on your Golden, don't. Dog hair has a different pH than human hair and needs a shampoo and conditioner specifically formulated for dogs. Gentle, moisturizing (look for a coconut oil base), tear-free dog shampoos are best. Conditioners serve the same purpose as coat sprays, and you may decide not to bother with conditioner at all—though it does make the initial post-bath comb-out easier.

Consider a Grooming Table

A grooming table is a sturdy metal table with a nonslip surface. It comes with a grooming arm—metal tubing from which a collar hangs that can help hold your dog still while you are grooming him. When your dog is on the table, *never leave his side;* he could hang himself if he tries to jump off.

The great thing about the grooming table is that it helps prevent strain on your back while grooming your Golden— once he is up on the table. The bad thing is trying to *get* your Golden up on the table in the first place. Lifting a sixty-plus pound dog in order to save strain on your back seems slightly contrary. You may decide to just get down on the floor to groom your Golden, but the table is worth considering.

Toothbrush and Toothpaste

Keep your Golden's teeth clean with a toothbrush and toothpaste made specifically for dogs. Dogs suffer from dental disease just as humans do. Plaque allowed to build up on your Golden's teeth leads to tooth decay, tooth loss, and infections that can wreck havoc on your Golden's health.

There are many styles of dog toothbrushes. The sort that slips over your finger like a little hood and has very soft bristles seems easiest to maneuver inside your dog's mouth, and massages the gums. It is also less likely to be chewed on because your dog will not want to bite hard on your finger.

The toothpaste you buy will be a tasty (to dogs!) flavor like liver, beef, or chicken. Never use human toothpaste on your dog; he cannot rinse, and it is unsafe to swallow.

Puppy Grooming

Other than when he transitions from his fuzzy puppy coat to the adult coat, there is not much need to groom your Golden puppy. Still, this is a great time to get him used to the process and to accepting daily handling. Later when he does need grooming or requires an examination at the vet, he'll be a pro at quietly accepting the attention. Dogs who are regularly groomed are very relaxed while being handled and touched, so this sort of practice is important.

Getting Started

If you are using a grooming table, place your Golden puppy up there every day for grooming practice. As he grows, you will need a walk-up ramp unless you are very strong. If you are grooming without a table, use a small rubber-backed throw rug on the floor to establish the boundaries of your grooming station.

Position him sitting, lying down, on his side, and standing, and systematically rub and massage his head, legs, back, feet, chest, and tummy using a slow, firm, circular motion with the pads of your fingers or thumbs. Follow these steps while holding his collar to prevent him from wriggling or jumping off, and to prohibit mouthing or biting. If he does bite, apply steady collar pressure by turning the collar to slightly rotate his head away from the hand he is biting. Don't scold or intimidate; let him figure things out through gentle cause and effect. When he relaxes, loosen your grip and keep speaking soothingly while massaging him. He will grow to love and accept this exercise, just as he once accepted similar attention from his mother, who cleaned and massaged him with her tongue.

Teach your Golden puppy to allow you to place your fingers inside his mouth by gently cupping his muzzle in one hand and sliding your forefinger under his lip, along the side of his gum. Next apply small massaging motions inside his cheeks, rubbing along both his gumline and the teeth on each side. When he gets used to this, you can introduce the finger toothbrush and toothpaste.

As your puppy improves at massage practice, you can progress to going over him with your grooming equipment, being sure to progress slowly and systematically. Start with your comb or bristle brush, just to get him familiar with the process. Move in the direction the hair grows, being sure to angle your comb toward his tail so you don't poke his skin.

While your puppy's fuzzy coat doesn't need much grooming, start getting him used to the process early on.

Check your Golden puppy's ears regularly, and even if they don't look dirty, get him used to having a cotton swab soaked in a little ear cleaner run around the inside of the ear (but never in the ear canal). Hold his paws and press and tap on his nails lightly to get him prepped for future nail trimming. He will get used to being examined and having sensitive parts of his body handled, and you will learn what is normal for your dog, making it easier to spot little problems before they require more serious attention. Your daily practice will pay off when your grown Golden has impeccable grooming manners.

Adult Grooming

You can groom your adult Golden daily and certainly no less than once a week. A heavily coated Golden with lots of feathering will need more upkeep than a dog with less coat and sparse feathers. The feathers of the front and rear legs, the tail feathers, and the fine hair just underneath and behind the ears are prone to matting due to scratching, chewing, or things getting caught in the longer hair. Combs are useful for the feathers and the area under the ears where mats collect.

Shedding

Goldens shed a bit all year round, but then go through a more extensive shedding of their coats twice a year. The timing depends on the climate in your area. When your dog sheds, his fine undercoat is lost *en masse,* often in clumps.

The fluffy feathering tends to mat and will need extra grooming attention.

During heavy shedding periods, you may wish to brush your dog several times a day to keep the fine undercoat from ending up all over your house and yard.

An application of grooming spray before you begin grooming will ease the removal of hair and reduce both static and floaters—airborne hairs you won't enjoy eating, inhaling, and being generally covered with. You can help loosen up that dead coat by running your hands and fingers through it and massaging the skin. You can also do this with your pin brush. Both help stimulate new coat growth and speed the shedding process.

The slicker brush will remove loose hair, and you can use your comb to remove the hair from your brushes if you can't just pull it out by hand. The slicker brush also is useful for removing tangles. Thinning shears can help break up mats so they can then be teased apart with a comb. If the mats are just too tightly bound, you can try to cut them in half and then work to salvage hair from the mat halves. In the worst case you may just have to carefully cut off the entire mat, being *very* careful not to cut your dog. Work the comb under the mat and then cut above the comb so there is no chance to get too close to your dog's skin.

Ear Cleaning

Your Golden's ears will need weekly cleaning. Even if they do not appear dirty, frequent care will prevent ear problems. Ear-cleaning solutions are available in pet supply stores. Place several drops in each ear and massage the ears for half a minute. This way the solution can penetrate the greasy dirt.

Let the dog shake his head to loosen the dirt. To actually remove the dirt, use cotton makeup pads. Swabs can damage the ear; *don't insert anything into your Golden's ear canal.* Clean the exterior areas of the inside of the ear, getting into the nooks and crannies of the outer ear.

If you dog needs more frequent ear cleanings, take him to the veterinarian. Redness, excessive head shaking, a strong odor, frequent ear scratching, and a dark discharge all are signs of ear infection or a foreign body in the ear. If you notice any of these signs, take your Golden to the vet.

Clean your dog's ears every week to prevent problems.

Bright Eyes

Your Golden's eyes, full of love and laughter, reflect his good health and give him a clear view of the world. Clear eye discharge is normal and can be wiped away from corners if there is a globby-looking buildup. Sometimes a murky film of mucus can cloud the eyes, and when this happens, you can carefully wipe it away. Don't touch the dog's eyeball, ever! Use a moistened corner of a cotton makeup pad at the inner corner of the eye, pulling the corner buildup of discharge toward the snout. Usually this will remove the attached mucus that was clouding your dog's eye. Greenish discharge indicates an infection and requires veterinary attention.

Brushing Teeth

Regular tooth brushing protects your Golden's good health. Calcium deposits accumulate primarily on the back upper molars but spread to all teeth but the incisors as dogs age. These deposits are known as *calculus* or *tartar* and are the leading cause of gum disease, which leads to eventual tooth loss. Daily brushings can slow down this process, but even regular brushing does not totally halt the formation of calculus.

To help prolong the health of your dog's mouth, he should have his teeth cleaned once a year at a veterinary clinic. Observing the mouth regularly and checking for abnormalities and broken teeth can lead to early detection of oral cancer or infection.

Regular tooth brushing will protect your dog's good health.

One of the worst enemies of a Golden's teeth is his habit of chewing on his coat. The coarse hairs wear down the front teeth. In many middle-aged to older dogs the incisors may even wear down to the gums. The only way to prevent this is to stop the dog from chewing his coat. If your dog develops a chronic coat-chewing problem, you may need to seek help from a behaviorist.

The Finishing Touches

The final grooming consideration for your Golden is trimming his hair. For this, the only thing you need is a pair of barber's scissors. The most obvious area to trim is your dog's feet, where he may grow an unnecessary amount of hair. The hair should be trimmed so that it is even around the edges of the pads along the outer edge and the bottom of the foot. Hair that sticks out between the toes may also be trimmed. It is not only neater, but the feet will track less dirt into the house and are easier to wipe clean. In the winter, the dog will be less likely to collect hard clumps of snow between his toes if this hair is kept trimmed.

If leg feathers are excessively long, you may want to trim them so they are less likely to bring in twigs, leaves, and other useless items. Some people trim the feathers quite short to make upkeep easier.

Many Goldens who have been spayed or neutered grow a longer-than-normal undercoat that extends beyond the outercoat. It is light and fluffy and is most prominent on the rear legs and shoulders. It often makes little mats or tangles and can require extra brushing. It is simple to trim this hair so that it is flush with the rest of the coat. This is not only more attractive, but also will mean less work for you.

Bathing Your Golden

Bathing is best done after the dog is brushed, rather than before, because wet knots can be really difficult to comb out. Goldens should be bathed no more than every six to eight weeks, and even this may be unnecessary on a shorter-coated dog who stays reasonably clean. Dirt from digging in the garden will brush right out as soon as it dries. However, Goldens do love to roll in smelly things when they get the chance, and if your dog prances into your home coated in muskrat poop, it is definitely bath time!

Excessive bathing can destroy the natural balance of oils in your Golden's skin and coat. There are exceptions: Certain skin conditions may warrant more frequent bathing with medicated shampoos.

New Products in the Fight Against Fleas

At one time, battling fleas meant exposing your dog and yourself to toxic dips, sprays, powders, and collars. But today there are flea preventives that work very well and are safe for your dog, you, and the environment. The two most common types are insect growth regulators (IGRs), which stop the immature flea from developing or maturing, and adult flea killers. To deal with an active infestation, experts usually recommend a product that has both.

These next-generation flea fighters generally come in one of two forms:

- **Topical treatments or spot-ons.** These products are applied to the skin, usually between the shoulder blades. The product is absorbed through the skin into the dog's system. Among the most widely available spot-ons are Advantage (kills adult fleas and larvae), Revolution (kills adult fleas), Frontline Plus (kills adult fleas and larvae, plus an IGR), K-9 Advantix (kills adult fleas and larvae), and BioSpot (kills adult fleas and larvae, plus an IGR).
- **Systemic products.** This is a pill your dog swallows that transmits a chemical throughout the dog's bloodstream. When a flea bites the dog, it picks up this chemical, which then prevents the flea's eggs from developing. Among the most widely available systemic products are Program (kills larvae only, plus an IGR) and Capstar (kills adult fleas).

Make sure you read all the labels and apply the products exactly as recommended, and that you check to make sure they are safe for puppies.

Lukewarm water is best, but cold water is fine if the weather is warm. Getting your Golden into the tub and keeping him there can be tricky. Your water-loving Golden who leaps willingly into lakes and streams may kick like a mule at the mere thought of entering a bathtub. You can help prevent this problem by having daily waterless bathtub visits for petting and treats. When real bath time rolls around, it will be less of a struggle.

In warm weather you may decide to bathe your Golden outdoors, using a small plastic wading pool and a hose with a spray head that lets you modify the water stream. Blasting your dog with a jet of icy water will not facilitate future bathing. You can put cotton balls dampened with a bit of baby oil in the ears to keep excess water out.

Diluted shampoo will go on and rinse off more easily. Use an empty gallon container and mix a small amount of shampoo with water and shake it around to create a solution. Wet your Golden thoroughly and then apply the diluted shampoo, making sure to keep it out of the dog's eyes and ears. Then rinse and rinse again. Be sure to get all the soap out by continuing to rinse even after all the soap appears to be gone.

If you wash your Golden with flea shampoo, remember that the suds must stay on the dog for several minutes before they are rinsed off. Flea shampoo only kills the fleas that are on your dog when he is being bathed. Topical monthly flea preventives are more effective (see the box on page 75); they don't just remove

In warm weather, you can bathe your dog outside.

fleas, they prevent them from coming back.

After your Golden's bath, towel
him off to remove excess water.
Most Goldens will shake wildly at
some time during and after the bath
and get you completely wet. If it is a
warm day, the dog can dry naturally. In colder weather, use a hand-
held hair dryer set at low heat.
Moving the dryer back and forth
with quick motions will help diffuse
the heat. Blow dry with your hand
against your dog's coat, fluffing the
hair so it dries more quickly—and
also gauging the heat to be sure
your dog isn't getting burned.

*Use a towel to remove excess water after a bath.
Don't let your dog get chilled.*

Once the dog is dry, run your
bristle brush over his coat to give him a fine finish, and then take a walk to show
off your beautiful Golden Retriever.

Don't Neglect the Nails

Trimming nails is essential for the health of your dog's feet. Dogs who get lots of
exercise or who walk on cement may wear their nails down on their own. But
even these dogs will require nail trimming as they become older and less active.
Normally, nails should be trimmed every two weeks or when they start to click
when the dog walks on hard surfaces. Long nails will scratch floors and get
caught in carpeting. Dogs can have difficulty walking on long nails. From a
health standpoint, nails that are allowed to become long for any period of time
will break down the structure of the foot by causing the toes to spread out and
splay the foot. Long nails are also more likely to split and require veterinary care.

The bundle of blood vessels and nerves running down the nail is called the
quick. If the tip of the quick is cut, it will bleed. Golden owners are fortunate,
because the breed's nails are light colored and somewhat opaque, and the
quick is visible when the nail is viewed from the side. To be safe, only cut the
hook part of the nail until you feel more confident. Most of the time a minor
cut to the quick will stop bleeding on its own. Styptic powder will also stop
the bleeding. If it doesn't, applying the powder along with some pressure does
the job.

Gently trim just a nail or two at a time when your Golden is a puppy, and he won't fuss about it as an adult.

Unless it is very sharp, the clipper may apply pressure that is scary to a puppy, and there is always a fear you might hit a vein. While this won't kill your dog, it will scare both of you. And a cut-too-short nail can hurt. If clipping nails is a scary proposition for you, most groomers and veterinary clinics will take care of it for a small fee.

You can desensitize your Golden to having his paws held and rubbed while you watch TV together, and then introduce nail filing with a large emery board or an electric nail grinder. Many Goldens sit politely for their "pawdicure" and never develop any resistance at all. As a bonus, filed nails have nice round tips that won't scratch skin or snag fabric.

Creepy Crawlies

While grooming and bathing your Golden, watch for signs of unwanted visitors: fleas, ticks, and mites. Any dog can pick up parasites, even those who live indoors in the finest homes and are walked in landscaped suburban or city areas. The little buggers lurk everywhere and can jump on any dog—even yours.

Fleas

Fleas are the most common cause of skin irritation for any dog, but Goldens are notoriously sensitive to skin irritants and tend to develop allergies to flea bites. Fleas also carry tapeworms. Fleas leap onto and feast upon a dog's blood, then drop off and lay their eggs in the environment.

Fleas are inclined to hang out on parts of your dog's body where he can't reach them with scratching—the back of the neck and especially around the tail base. Look for little black flecks (flea poop) and reddish irritation as signs your dog has picked up passengers. Extreme irritation will require veterinary attention, and some dogs develop skin infections in response to fleabites.

Where there is one flea, there are many, so you must treat more than just your dog if you want them to be gone for good. Household flea treatments that contain growth inhibitors will stunt hatching fleas and not allow them to develop into adults, thus breaking their life cycle. Topical preventives for every pet in the home, as well as washing or treating all bedding, furniture, and carpets, will end the infestation. Keeping your dog protected with a monthly, topical flea preventive will stop a flea problem from ever getting started.

Ticks

Check your dog for ticks every time you groom him. This is where daily grooming examinations can be extra important. Deer ticks pose a health risk to both humans and dogs because they carry the Lyme disease spirochete. Studies have shown that an infected tick normally cannot begin transmitting the spirochete until it has been attached to its host about thirty-six to forty-eight hours—reinforcing the need for daily examinations!

Deer ticks are gray rather than brown and are common in both suburban and rural areas, especially in the northeast. The first sign of Lyme disease is a telltale bulls-eye rash that extends in a circle from the bite. This can be hard to see on a

Fleas and ticks lurk everywhere outside. Goldens tend to have flea allergies, so use flea-and-tick preventives to keep your dog safe.

Making Your Environment Flea Free

If there are fleas on your dog, there are fleas in your home, yard, and car, even if you can't see them. Take these steps to combat them.

In your home:

- Wash whatever is washable (the dog bed, sheets, blankets, pillow covers, slipcovers, curtains, etc.).
- Vacuum everything else in your home—furniture, floors, rugs, everything. Pay special attention to the folds and crevices in upholstery, cracks between floorboards, and the spaces between the floor and the baseboards. Flea larvae are sensitive to sunlight, so inside the house they prefer deep carpet, bedding, and cracks and crevices.
- When you're done, throw the vacuum cleaner bag away—in an outside garbage can.
- Use a nontoxic flea-killing powder, such as Flea Busters or Zodiac FleaTrol, to treat your carpets (but remember, it does not control fleas elsewhere in the house). The powder stays deep in the carpet and kills fleas (using a form of boric acid) for up to a year.
- If you have a particularly serious flea problem, consider using a fogger or long-lasting spray to kill any adult and larval fleas, or having a professional exterminator treat your home.

Golden. Following that first sign, the dog may exhibit fever, staggering, weakness, and swelling of the joints. Lyme disease can end in severe arthritis and heart problems.

Ticks must be removed from your dog with tweezers, but they bury their heads in your dog's skin, and it can be difficult to get the head with the body (see the box on page 82). Choose smooth (no rasps), fine-point tweezers whose tips align tightly when pressed firmly together. If you remove a tick, consider placing it in a small container for later examination. Call your veterinarian to determine if there is someplace locally where the tick can be tested. Monitor the bite site, and if you notice any symptoms, have your Golden examined by a veterinarian as soon as possible.

In your car:

- Take out the floor mats and hose them down with a strong stream of water, then hang them up to dry in the sun.
- Wash any towels, blankets, or other bedding you regularly keep in the car.
- Thoroughly vacuum the entire interior of your car, paying special attention to the seams between the bottom and back of the seats.
- When you're done, throw the vacuum cleaner bag away—in an outside garbage can.

In your yard:

- Flea larvae prefer shaded areas that have plenty of organic material and moisture, so rake the yard thoroughly and bag all the debris in tightly sealed bags.
- Spray your yard with an insecticide that has residual activity for at least thirty days. Insecticides that use a form of boric acid are nontoxic. Some newer products contain an insect growth regulator (such as fenoxycarb) and need to be applied only once or twice a year.
- For an especially difficult flea problem, consider having an exterminator treat your yard.
- Keep your yard free of piles of leaves, weeds, and other organic debris. Be especially careful in shady, moist areas, such as under bushes.

Mites

If your Golden is scratching and you cannot determine the cause, he may have an infestation of mites. Mites are microscopic creatures that burrow into the skin to lay their eggs. This causes intense itching, and your dog will chew and bite at his skin. There are several types of mites that infest dogs' skin, causing various forms of mange.

Cheyletiella mange, also known as walking dandruff, is characterized by flakes of skin that result when the mites hatch from under your dog's skin, dislodging a skin flake. Demodectic mange is passed to puppies from their mom. The pups may carry it without symptoms unless they suffer from immune-system stress, at which time they may experience flare-ups. Sarcoptic, or red mange, is the most serious and most difficult to treat. It is also contagious.

How to Get Rid of a Tick

Although the new generation of flea fighters are partially effective in killing ticks once they are on your dog, they are not 100 percent effective and will not keep ticks from biting your dog in the first place. During tick season (which, depending on where you live, can be spring, summer, and/or fall), examine your dog every day for ticks. Pay particular attention to your dog's neck, behind the ears, the armpits, and the groin.

When you find a tick, use a pair of tweezers to grasp the tick as close as possible to the dog's skin and pull it out using firm, steady pressure. Check to make sure you get the whole tick (mouth parts left in your dog's skin can cause an infection), then wash the wound and dab it with some antibiotic ointment. Watch for signs of inflammation.

Ticks carry very serious diseases that are transmittable to humans, so dispose of the tick safely. *Never* crush it between your fingers. Don't flush it down the toilet either, because the tick will survive the trip and infect another animal. Instead, use the tweezers to place the tick in a tight-sealing jar or plastic dish with a little alcohol, put on the lid, and dispose of the container in an outdoor garbage can. Wash the tweezers thoroughly with hot water and alcohol.

Any suspicion of mites should send you to the vet, who will look at scrapings from your dog's skin under a microscope to determine if there are any mites present. Treatments vary depending on the type of mite and the severity of the symptoms. Talk to your veterinarian about treating the environment to prevent reinfestation.

Chapter 8

Keeping Your Golden Healthy

Keeping your Golden Retriever healthy from the day you meet her until the day you must finally say goodbye is your greatest and most rewarding responsibility. The strongest body and soundest genetic background are not enough to give your Golden a healthy life. She also needs your attentive care.

A Healthy Start

The first time you visit your veterinarian with your new Golden, it should be as a social visit to help acclimate her to the environment and to introduce this very important person who will be a part of the rest of her life. Be friendly and calm and as relaxed as possible, to create a model for your Golden. Give your vet a toy or treat to hold and then hand to your dog with his or her scent on it. Your Golden's first visit also offers an opportunity for you to ask any questions about feeding, schedules, or health.

Your dog's breeder will have given your Golden puppy her first shots and will have explained when her next set of vaccinations is due. Schedule your second visit to the vet to coincide with her vaccination due date. Bring a small stool sample to have it checked for parasites.

Hereditary Diseases

Despite all our care and attention, Golden Retrievers do occasionally suffer from conditions to which the breed seems to be predisposed. Of course, not all Goldens have these problems. But some do. Good breeders carefully screen and test their dogs for all known genetic problems before breeding them. Unfortunately, problems can pop up in even the best Golden Retriever lines. Hopefully, you will never encounter any of the following problems, but you should be aware of what they are and some of their symptoms.

Cataracts

There are several types of cataracts that affect Goldens. They are characterized by the part of the lens on which they appear and the age of the dog. Most are genetic, but others can be caused by injury or the aging process. Most cataracts are nonprogressive in Goldens, and vision impairment is usually mild. Diagnosis must be made by a veterinary ophthalmologist.

Your veterinarian will help you set up a regular schedule of examinations and vaccinations for your dog

Epilepsy

Genetic epilepsy usually appears before 3 years of age. The older-onset form of epilepsy may have a genetic predisposition. These are seizures that occur regularly and follow a typical pattern. Epilepsy can be controlled by daily medication.

Hip Dysplasia

Hip dysplasia is a malformation of the ball-and-socket joint of the hips that can affect one or both sides of the dog. As some dogs age, these joints wear down, and the ball of the head of the femur begins to fit incorrectly into the hip socket. The resulting laxity in the joint causes more degeneration, as well as bone spurs which are very painful. Arthritis is also associated with the disease.

The incidence of many of the orthopedic problems that plague Goldens can be minimized with careful, responsible breeding.

Hip dysplasia can only be properly diagnosed using special X-rays. Mild to moderately dysplastic dogs can lead normal lives as long as they're kept in good weight and physical condition. Appropriate exercise, especially swimming, will help a dysplastic dog lead a normal life. Pain can be relieved with anti-inflammatory drugs and painkillers prescribed by your veterinarian. In extreme cases, surgery may have to be performed to replace or remove the hip.

Hypothyroidism

Hypothyroidism (underactive thyroid) may be genetic and is also associated with a poor immune system. There may be physical signs such as weight gain, lethargy, poor coat, infertility in both sexes, and longer than normal time between heat cycles in intact females. A thyroid test will show if there is a problem. Daily medication prescribed by your vet will correct low thyroid levels.

Lymphosarcoma

This form of cancer, which affects the lymph system, sometimes occurs in Goldens, who may be genetically predisposed to it. Lymphosarcoma is linked to autoimmune problems. Symptoms include poor appetite, lethargy, and chronically swollen peripheral lymph nodes, which are located under the dog's

Vaccines

What vaccines dogs need and how often they need them has been a subject of controversy for several years. Researchers, healthcare professionals, vaccine manufacturers, and dog owners do not always agree on which vaccines each dog needs or how often booster shots must be given.

In 2006, the American Animal Hospital Association issued a set of vaccination guidelines and recommendations intended to help dog owners and veterinarians sort through much of the controversy and conflicting information. The guidelines designate four vaccines as *core*, or essential, for every dog, because of the serious nature of the diseases and their widespread distribution. These are canine distemper virus (using a modified live virus or recombinant modified live virus vaccine), canine parvovirus (using a modified live virus vaccine), canine adenovirus-2 (using a modified live virus vaccine), and rabies (using a killed virus). The general recommendations for their administration (except rabies, for which you must follow local laws) are:

- Vaccinate puppies at 6–8 weeks, 9–11 weeks, and 12–14 weeks.
- Give an initial "adult" vaccination when the dog is older than 16 weeks; two doses, three to four weeks apart, are

jawbone, on the chest, and on the upper back side of the hind legs. Chemotherapy treatment can prolong the life of a dog with cancer, but it is not curative.

Osteochondritis Dissecans

This disease, caused by faulty cartilage lining the ends of the long bones, affects the shoulder joints and sometimes the hocks (the collection of bones at the bottom third of the dog's back legs that are the equivalent of human heels) and stifles (the curving equivalent of human knees on the front of a dog's back legs). As an affected dog exercises, the cartilage is increasingly damaged. Goldens appear

advised, but one dose is considered protective and acceptable.

- Give a booster shot when the dog is 1 year old.
- Give a subsequent booster shot every three years, unless there are risk factors that make it necessary to vaccinate more or less often.

Noncore vaccines should only be considered for those dogs who risk exposure to a particular disease because of geographic area, lifestyle, frequency of travel, or other issues. They include vaccines against distemper-measles virus, canine parainfluenza virus, leptospirosis, Bordetella bronchiseptica, and Borrelia burgdorferi (Lyme disease).

Vaccines that are not generally recommended because the disease poses little risk to dogs or is easily treatable, or the vaccine has not been proven to be effective, are those against giardia, canine coronavirus, and canine adenovirus-1.

Often, combination injections are given to puppies, with one shot containing several core and noncore vaccines. Your veterinarian may be reluctant to use separate shots that do not include the noncore vaccines, because they must be specially ordered. If you are concerned about these noncore vaccines, talk to your vet.

to have a genetic predisposition to this problem, which is diagnosed by X-ray. In mild cases it will heal with rest, but more serious cases usually require surgery.

Progressive Retinal Atrophy

Progressive retinal atrophy (PRA) is a gradual degeneration of the cells of the retina. It first occurs in middle-aged dogs and leads to loss of vision. This is less common in Goldens than cataracts, but it still occurs. CERF (the Canine Eye Registry Foundation) was established to register dogs whose eyes test free of genetic problems.

Why Spay and Neuter?

Breeding dogs is a serious undertaking that should only be part of a well-planned breeding program. Why? Because dogs pass on their physical and behavioral problems to their offspring. Even healthy, well-behaved dogs can pass on problems in their genes.

Is your dog so sweet that you'd like to have a litter of puppies just like her? If you breed her to another dog, the pups will not have the same genetic heritage she has. Breeding her *parents* again will increase the odds of a similar pup, but even then, the puppies in the second litter could inherit different genes. In fact, *there is no way to breed a dog to be just like another dog.*

Meanwhile, thousands and thousands of dogs are killed in animal shelters every year simply because they have no homes. Casual breeding is a big contributor to this problem.

If you don't plan to breed your dog, is it still a good idea to spay her or neuter him? Yes!

When you spay your female:

- You avoid her heat cycles, during which she discharges blood and scent.
- It greatly reduces the risk of mammary cancer and eliminates the risk of *pyometra* (an often fatal infection of the uterus) and uterine cancer.
- It prevents unwanted pregnancies.
- It reduces dominance behaviors and aggression.

When you neuter your male:

- It curbs the desire to roam and to fight with other males.
- It greatly reduces the risk of prostate cancer and eliminates the risk of testicular cancer.
- It helps reduce leg lifting and mounting behavior.
- It reduces dominance behaviors and aggression.

Skin Allergies and Hot Spots

Golden Retrievers have a predisposition to skin allergies, indicated by scratching excessively and self-chewing, especially the paws. Although allergies have a genetic basis, diet and environment play a role, too.

The Golden's thick undercoat, especially if it frequently stays damp, is an excellent environment for the development of hot spots. Hot spots are surface skin infections that occur when normal skin bacteria grow and become resistant to the body's natural defenses. Hot spots are swollen, inflamed patches that can cause pain and itching, and may exude smelly pus.

Any excessive scratching or signs of skin irritation should be examined by your vet. Medications can be prescribed and diet can be modified, which may help reduce skin irritations and allergy symptoms.

Subaortic Stenosis

This is a genetically caused defect in the valve ring below the aorta of the heart. It is detected by a murmur, and accurate diagnosis is made using a variety of advanced techniques including an echocardiogram. In cases of minor murmurs, a dog should lead a normal though sedate life. Dogs with severe grades of

As dogs age, they experience a number of physical changes. More frequent veterinary checkups will help you monitor your older dog's health.

stenosis will show physical signs and often die unexpectedly at a young age. Diagnosis should be made by a veterinary cardiologist.

Von Willebrand's Disease

This is a genetic clotting disorder that may be suspected if it takes longer than normal for a wound to stop bleeding. A blood test is necessary to diagnose this disease.

Common Canine Ailments

Anal Glands

Dogs have anal sacs, which are located under the skin on both sides of the anal opening and are full of thin, smelly, brown fluid. They should be checked periodically. When the sacs are impacted (blocked), they become swollen, and the fluid is very dark and viscous. Serious impaction can lead to infection and require surgery.

Needless to say, impacted anal sacs are quite uncomfortable for the dog. That discomfort leads to butt scooting—your dog in a sitting position scooting across floors to wipe the uncomfortable anus on your floor. So, while the thought of draining—known as *expressing*—the fluid from the anal sacs sounds incredibly gross to some, the thought of leaving the dog to express them on your floor is gross to all.

You can express the sacs yourself. A good time to do it is during your dog's bath. The sacs are expressed by placing the thumb and the index and third fingers of one hand on both sides of the outer edge of the anus. Strong inward-squeezing pressure on both sides of the anus at the same time usually removes the smelly contents of the sac. A paper towel should be kept in the hand that is squeezing to collect the fluid. If you are too horrified at the thought, bring your dog to the vet or a groomer.

There is no way to breed a dog who is just like another dog.

Bloat

Bloat, or acute gastric dilatation, occurs when gas becomes trapped in a dog's stomach and cannot be released. Without immediate medical attention, bloating dogs will go into shock and die. When a dog eats a large amount of food at one time, the risk of bloat may be increased. Some people believe that soaking their dog's kibbles in water to expand them and release any trapped gases before feeding reduces bloat risk.

Bloat tends to affect large breeds with broad chests. It is a serious emergency.

A dog with bloat will appear restless and uncomfortable. She may drool and attempt to vomit. Her abdomen will appear swollen, and the area will be painful. In severe cases, the stomach actually twists on itself in a condition called gastric torsion. If this happens, the dog will go into shock due to the lack of blood supply to the stomach and spleen. *Bloat is an emergency!* The dog must be rushed to the vet.

Diarrhea

Diarrhea is very loose to watery stools that your dog has difficulty controlling. It can be caused by something as simple as changing her diet, a change in water, or a parasite infection. If diarrhea is bloody or has a very offensive odor, especially combined with vomiting and fevers, it is most likely a virus and requires immediate veterinary attention.

Heartworm

Heartworm is found in every part of North America and is spread by mosquitoes. The mosquito's bite injects heartworm microfilaria (larvae) that develop into worms six to twelve inches long. As these worms mature, they take up residence in the dog's heart, clogging it and resulting in the dog's death.

The symptoms of heartworm include coughing, tiring easily, difficulty breathing, and weight loss. Treatment for heartworm is very expensive and very dangerous.

Heartworm can be prevented with medication given once per month during warm months, and in some areas all year round. As a side benefit, the

Outdoor lakes and streams harbor internal parasites, including the mosquitoes that carry heartworm.

heartworm preventive also kills all other internal worms except tapeworms. The preventive won't cure an existing heartworm infection and shouldn't be given to dogs whose blood hasn't been tested to confirm they are heartworm-free.

Internal Parasites

The inside of a dog's body may become inhabited by a variety of parasites. Most of these are in the worm family: tapeworms, roundworms, whipworms, and hookworms all plague our canine friends. There are also several types of protozoa, mainly coccidia and giardia, that cause problems. Luckily, these pests are less of a problem for modern dogs, thanks to routine veterinary care and preventive medications.

If you do notice a dull coat, weight loss, diarrhea, or worms in your dog's stool, see your vet for treatment. Do not use over-the-counter wormers because they may not treat the type of worms your dog has.

Lameness

Puppy and adolescent Goldens are prone to growth-related limping caused by an inflammation of the long bones, known as panosteitis. It can be controlled with rest, a diet that doesn't rush a puppy's growth, and in some cases anti-inflammatory drugs from your veterinarian. A limp that appears from nowhere and gets progressively worse is cause for concern.

A serious concern with lameness, especially as a dog ages, is bone cancer. This can only be confirmed by tests and X-rays.

Vomiting

Any sort of stomach irritation may result in your Golden vomiting, which is perfectly natural for dogs. In fact, she may deliberately eat coarse grass to induce vomiting if she has an upset stomach. Sometimes dogs throw up an uncomfortable buildup of stomach acid, which has a frothy yellow appearance. Repeated vomiting can be a symptom of a more serious problem, such as an intestinal blockage. Dark-colored, bloody, or foul-colored vomit all indicate an underlying health problem that should be diagnosed by your veterinarian. If your Golden ever vomits repeatedly or becomes unable to keep down her food, a visit to the veterinarian is also in order.

What to Do in an Emergency

Hopefully, your Golden will never have a serious injury or illness, but there are some first-aid measures you will want to know.

A dog in extreme pain may bite if touched. As a precaution, her mouth should be restrained with some type of muzzle. A rope, a pair of pantyhose, or a strip of cloth about two feet long all work in a pinch. First tie a loose knot that has an opening large enough to easily fit around the dog's muzzle. Tie the knot on the top of the muzzle. Then bring the two ends down and tie another knot underneath the dog's chin. Finally, pull the ends behind the head and tie a knot below the ears. Don't do this if there is an injury to the dog's head or if she requires artificial respiration. And make sure she has room to breathe.

Even the sweetest, most loving dog may bite when she is frightened or in pain. In an emergency, handle your dog with caution.

When to Call the Veterinarian

Go to the vet right away or take your dog to an emergency veterinary clinic if:

- Your dog is choking
- Your dog is having trouble breathing
- Your dog has been injured and you cannot stop the bleeding within a few minutes
- Your dog has been stung or bitten by an insect and the site is swelling
- Your dog has been bitten by a snake
- Your dog has been bitten by another animal (including a dog) and shows any swelling or bleeding
- Your dog has touched, licked, or in any way been exposed to a poison
- Your dog has been burned by either heat or caustic chemicals
- Your dog has been hit by a car
- Your dog has any obvious broken bones or cannot put any weight on one of her limbs
- Your dog has a seizure

Make an appointment to see the vet as soon as possible if:

- Your dog has been bitten by a cat, another dog, or a wild animal
- Your dog has been injured and is still limping an hour later

Artificial Respiration

Situations that may cause unconsciousness include drowning, choking, electric shock, or traumatic shock. In these cases your Golden may stop breathing. The first thing to do is check the mouth and air passages for any object that might obstruct breathing. If you find nothing, or once the airway has been cleared, hold the dog's mouth closed while covering the nose completely with your mouth. Gently exhale into the dog's nose. This should be done at ten to twelve breaths per minute.

> **TIP**
>
> Know where the nearest 24-hour emergency veterinary clinic is located. Emergency phone numbers should be posted where they can be easily located.

- Your dog has unexplained swelling or redness
- Your dog's appetite changes
- Your dog vomits repeatedly and can't seem to keep food down, or drools excessively while eating
- You see any changes in your dog's urination or defecation (pain during elimination, change in regular habits, blood in urine or stool, diarrhea, foul-smelling stool)
- Your dog scoots her rear end on the floor
- Your dog's energy level, attitude, or behavior changes for no apparent reason
- Your dog has crusty or cloudy eyes, or excessive tearing or discharge
- Your dog's nose is dry or chapped, hot, crusty, or runny
- Your dog's ears smell foul, have a dark discharge, or seem excessively waxy
- Your dog's gums are inflamed or bleeding, her teeth look brown, or her breath is foul
- Your dog's skin is red, flaky, itchy, or inflamed, or she keeps chewing at certain spots
- Your dog's coat is dull, dry, brittle, or bare in spots
- Your dog's paws are red, swollen, tender, cracked, or the nails are split or too long
- Your dog is panting excessively, wheezing, unable to catch her breath, breathing heavily, or sounds strange when she breathes

Choking

Small objects such as balls, sticks, bits of rawhide, and pieces of torn-up toys can get caught in your dog's throat. If your dog has problems breathing accompanied by coughing or gagging, it may be a sign that an air passage is blocked. Check for an object lodged in your dog's throat, and if you see it, try to hook it with your forefinger. If you can't remove it, try elevating her rear end and striking her with the palm of your hand between her shoulder blades.

If that fails to dislodge the object, use the Heimlich maneuver. Place your dog on her side and, using both hands with palms down, apply quick thrusts to the abdomen just below the dog's last rib. If your dog won't lie down, grasp either side of the end of the rib cage and squeeze in short thrusts. Make a sharp enough movement to cause the air in the lungs to force the object out. If the cause cannot be found or removed, professional help is needed.

How to Make a Canine First-Aid Kit

If your dog hurts herself, even a minor cut, it can be very upsetting for both of you. Having a first-aid kit handy will help you to help her, calmly and efficiently. What should be in your canine first-aid kit?

- Antibiotic ointment
- Antiseptic and antibacterial cleansing wipes
- Benadryl
- Cotton-tipped applicators
- Disposable razor
- Elastic wrap bandages
- Extra leash and collar
- First-aid tape of various widths
- Gauze bandage roll
- Gauze pads of different sizes, including eye pads
- Hydrogen peroxide
- Instant cold compress
- Kaopectate tablets or liquid
- Latex gloves
- Lubricating jelly
- Muzzle
- Nail clippers
- Pen, pencil, and paper for notes and directions
- Pepto-Bismol
- Round-ended scissors and pointy scissors
- Safety pins
- Sterile saline eyewash
- Thermometer (rectal)
- Tweezers

Dog Bites

Any dog, even your gregarious Golden, can wind up in a tussle with another dog, especially if they are both intact (not neutered) adults of the same gender. If your Golden gets bitten by another dog, she will need to have her wound irrigated, an antiseptic and topical antibiotic applied, and she may even require oral antibiotics. Only very drastic dog bites are stitched, because closing the wound increases the risk of infection. All but the most minor bite wounds should be treated by your veterinarian.

Electric Shock

A chewing puppy who finds and gnaws on electrical cords is in for a shock—of the electrical sort—if her teeth reach the wire inside the cord. The shock can be so severe she may be killed instantly, or she may be knocked unconscious and stop breathing. If she is not breathing, try artificial respiration as described on page 94.

Heatstroke

Heatstroke occurs when a dog's body temperature greatly exceeds the normal 101.5 degrees F. It can be caused by overexertion in warm temperatures, but the most common cause is leaving a dog in a closed vehicle. A dog should *never* be left in a closed car, even in the shade.

A dog suffering from heatstroke will feel hot to the touch and have short, shallow, rapid breaths. Saliva may bubble from her mouth, and her heartbeat will be very fast. Shock is a possible side effect of heatstroke, and the dog must be cooled immediately by wetting her down with cool water in any way that is available. She should have

Be sensible in the warm weather. Exercise your dog at dusk and dawn and help her keep cool. This dog has a bowl full of ice cubes.

small amounts of water placed in her mouth and then be dried and wrapped in cool, damp towels and taken to her veterinarian at once. Back at home she should be allowed to rest in a cool place for the next several hours.

Hypothermia

Hypothermia occurs when a dog is exposed to extreme cold for long periods. Symptoms include violent shivering, a tummy that is very cold to the touch, and stiff, slow movement. Your Golden may become hypothermic if she swims in icy water or stays outside in cold weather for too long. Her body temperature will drop, she will become chilled, and she may go into shock.

The hypothermic dog should be placed in a warm environment and wrapped in towels or blankets. If she is already wet, a warm bath can help. Massaging her body will help increase the circulation to normal levels. If you are outdoors and

Even with their abundant coats, with prolonged exposure Goldens can sometimes get too cold.

your dog becomes hypothermic, you may need to hold her against your body and wrap your jacket around her until she warms up enough to transport home.

Insect Bites

The seriousness of reactions to insect bites varies. The affected area will be red, swollen, and painful. In the case of bee stings, the stinger should always be removed. Locate the translucent stinger by finding the swollen area and looking at its center from different angles. Once you spot the stinger, pull it straight out using tweezers. A paste made of baking soda can be applied to the wound, and ice should be applied to the area to relieve swelling. The bites of some spiders, centipedes, and scorpions can cause severe illness and lead to shock. Dogs may show allergic symptoms such as hives, facial swelling, and difficulty breathing, all of which must be treated by a veterinarian.

Poison

In the case of poisoning, the only thing to do is get help immediately. If you know the source of the poison, take the container or object with you, as this will aid treatment. Common sources of poisoning in dogs include antifreeze, chocolate, cleaning solvents, disinfectants, houseplants, insecticides, slug bait, mouse and rat poison, pine-oil cleaners, soaps, and detergents. Symptoms of poisoning include vomiting, convulsions, lack of coordination, and collapse. Some poisons work fast and can kill your dog quickly. If you suspect poisoning, get to the vet immediately.

ASPCA Animal Poison Control Center

The ASPCA Animal Poison Control Center has a staff of licensed veterinarians and board-certified toxicologists available 24 hours a day, 365 days a year. The number to call is (888) 426-4435. You will be charged a consultation fee of $60 per case, charged to most major credit cards. There is no charge for follow-up calls in critical cases. At your request, they will also contact your veterinarian. Specific treatment and information can be provided via fax. Put the number in large, legible print with your other emergency telephone numbers. Be prepared to give your name, address, and phone number; what your dog has gotten into (the amount and how long ago); your dog's breed, age, sex, and weight; and what signs and symptoms the dog is showing. You can log onto www.aspca.org and click on "Animal Poison Control Center" for more information, including a list of toxic and nontoxic plants.

Shock

Whenever a dog is injured or is seriously ill, there is a risk she will go into shock—a state of collapse and circulatory shutdown in response to trauma. A dog in shock will be listless, weak, and cold to the touch. Her gums will be pale. If not treated, a dog will die from shock even if the illness or injuries that caused it are not fatal. A dog in shock needs immediate veterinary care. The dog should be kept as comfortable and warm as possible on the way to the clinic.

Traumatic Injury

The first concern following traumatic injury is to stabilize the dog and to stop bleeding. Cuts and wounds should be covered with bandaging material or a clean cloth; apply direct pressure. If a dog has been injured or is too ill to walk on her own, she will have to be carried. Keep the dog's body as flat and still as possible. Two people are usually needed to move a large dog, who should be carried on a piece of plywood, a blanket held taut, or anything else that can be used as a stretcher.

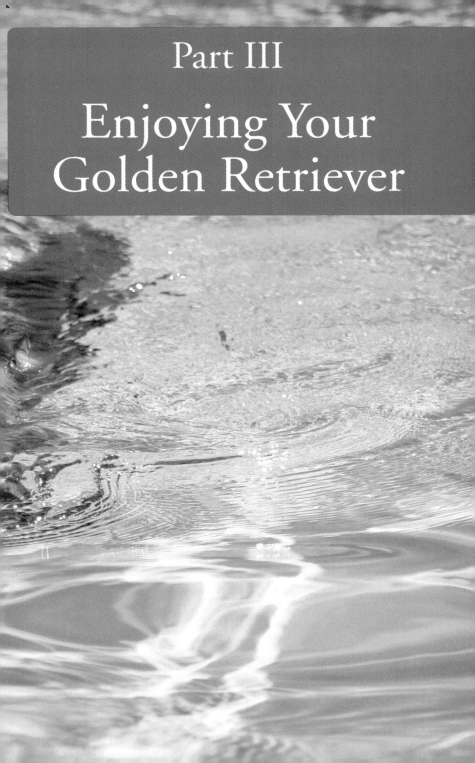

Part III
Enjoying Your Golden Retriever

Chapter 9

Training Your Golden Retriever

by Peggy Moran

Training makes your best friend better! A properly trained dog has a happier life and a longer life expectancy. He is also more appreciated by the people he encounters each day, both at home and out and about.

A trained dog walks nicely and joins his family often, going places untrained dogs cannot go. He is never rude or unruly, and he always happily comes when called. When he meets people for the first time, he greets them by sitting and waiting to be petted, rather than jumping up. At home he doesn't compete with his human family, and alone he is not destructive or overly anxious. He isn't continually nagged with words like "no," since he has learned not to misbehave in the first place. He is never shamed, harshly punished, or treated unkindly, and he is a well-loved, involved member of the family.

Sounds good, doesn't it? If you are willing to invest some time, thought, and patience, the words above could soon be used to describe your dog (though perhaps changing "he" to "she"). Educating your pet in a positive way is fun and easy, and there is no better gift you can give your pet than the guarantee of improved understanding and a great relationship.

This chapter will explain how to offer kind leadership, reshape your pet's behavior in a positive and practical way, and even get a head start on simple obedience training.

Understanding Builds the Bond

Dog training is a learning adventure on both ends of the leash. Before attempting to teach their dog new behaviors or change unwanted ones, thoughtful dog owners take the time to understand why their pets behave the way they do, and how their own behavior can be either a positive or negative influence on their dog.

Canine Nature

Loving dogs as much as we do, it's easy to forget they are a completely different species. Despite sharing our homes and living as appreciated members of our families, dogs do not think or learn exactly the same way people do. Even if you love your dog like a child, you must remember to respect the fact that he is actually a dog.

Dogs have no idea when their behavior is inappropriate from a human perspective. They are not aware of the value of possessions they chew or of messes they make or the worry they sometimes seem to cause. While people tend to look at behavior as good and bad or right and wrong, dogs just discover what works and what doesn't work. Then they behave accordingly, learning from their own experiences and increasing or reducing behaviors to improve results for themselves.

You might wonder, "But don't dogs want to please us"? My answer is yes, provided your pleasure reflects back to them in positive ways they can feel and appreciate. Dogs do things for *dog* reasons, and everything they do works for them in some way or they wouldn't be doing it!

The Social Dog

Our pets descended from animals who lived in tightly knit, cooperative social groups. Though far removed in appearance and lifestyle from their ancestors, our dogs still relate in many of the same ways their wild relatives did. And in their relationships with one another, wild canids either lead or follow.

Canine ranking relationships are not about cruelty and power; they are about achievement and abilities. Competent dogs with high levels of drive and confidence step up, while deferring dogs step aside. But followers don't get the short end of the stick; they benefit from the security of having a more competent dog at the helm.

Our domestic dogs still measure themselves against other members of their group—us! Dog owners whose actions lead to positive results have willing, secure followers. But dogs may step up and fill the void or cut loose and do their own thing when their people fail to show capable leadership. When dogs are pushy, aggressive, and rude, or independent and unwilling, it's not because they have designs on the role of "master." It is more likely their owners failed to provide consistent leadership.

Dogs in training benefit from their handler's good leadership. Their education flows smoothly because they are impressed. Being in charge doesn't require you to physically dominate or punish your dog. You simply need to make some subtle changes in the way you relate to him every day.

Lead Your Pack!

Create schedules and structure daily activities. Dogs are creatures of habit and routines will create security. Feed meals at the same times each day and also try to schedule regular walks, training practices, and toilet outings. Your predictability will help your dog be patient.

Ask your dog to perform a task. Before releasing him to food or freedom, have him do something as simple as sit on command. Teach him that cooperation earns great results!

Give a release prompt (such as "let's go") when going through doors leading outside. This is a better idea than allowing your impatient pup to rush past you.

Pet your dog when he is calm, not when he is excited. Turn your touch into a tool that relaxes and settles.

Reward desirable rather than inappropriate behavior. Petting a jumping dog (who hasn't been invited up) reinforces jumping. Pet sitting dogs, and only invite lap dogs up after they've first "asked" by waiting for your invitation.

Replace personal punishment with positive reinforcement. Show a dog what *to do,* and motivate him to want to do it, and there will be no need to punish him for what he should *not do.* Dogs naturally follow, without the need for force or harshness.

Play creatively and appropriately. Your dog will learn the most about his social rank when he is playing with you. During play, dogs work to control toys and try to get the best of one another in a friendly way. The wrong sorts of play can create problems: For example, tug of war can lead to aggressiveness. Allowing your dog to control toys during play may result in possessive guarding when he has something he really values, such as a bone. Dogs who are chased during play may later run away from you when you approach to leash them. The right kinds of play will help increase your dog's social confidence while you gently assert your leadership.

How Dogs Learn (and How They Don't)

Dog training begins as a meeting of minds—yours and your dog's. Though the end goal may be to get your dog's body to behave in a specific way, training starts as a mind game. Your dog is learning all the time by observing the consequences of his actions and social interactions. He is always seeking out what he perceives as desirable and trying to avoid what he perceives as undesirable.

He will naturally repeat a behavior that either brings him more good stuff or makes bad stuff go away (these are both types of reinforcement). He will naturally avoid a behavior that brings him more bad stuff or makes the good stuff go away (these are both types of punishment).

Both reinforcement and punishment can be perceived as either the direct result of something the dog did himself, or as coming from an outside source.

Using Life's Rewards

Your best friend is smart and he is also cooperative. When the best things in life can only be had by working with you, your dog will view you as a facilitator. You unlock doors to all of the positively reinforcing experiences he values: his freedom, his friends at the park, food, affection, walks, and play. The trained dog accompanies you through those doors and waits to see what working with you will bring.

Rewarding your dog for good behavior is called positive reinforcement, and, as we've just seen, it increases the likelihood that he will repeat that behavior. The perfect reward is anything your dog wants that is safe and appropriate. Don't limit yourself to toys, treats, and things that come directly from you. Harness life's positives—barking at squirrels, chasing a falling leaf, bounding away from you at the dog park, pausing for a moment to sniff everything—and allow your dog to earn access to those things as rewards that come from cooperating with you. When he looks at you, when he sits, when he comes when you call—any prompted behavior can earn one of life's rewards. When he works with you, he earns the things he most appreciates; but when he tries to get those things on his own, he cannot. Rather than seeing you as someone who always says "no," your dog will view you as the one who says "let's go!" He will *want* to follow.

What About Punishment?

Not only is it unnecessary to personally punish dogs, it is abusive. No matter how convinced you are that your dog "knows right from wrong," in reality he will associate personal punishment with the punisher. The resulting cowering, "guilty"-looking postures are actually displays of submission and fear. Later,

Purely Positive Reinforcement

With positive training, we emphasize teaching dogs what they should do to earn reinforcements, rather than punishing them for unwanted behaviors.

- Focus on teaching "do" rather than "don't." For example, a sitting dog isn't jumping.
- Use positive reinforcers that are valuable to your dog and the situation: A tired dog values rest; a confined dog values freedom.
- Play (appropriately)!
- Be a consistent leader.
- Set your dog up for success by anticipating and preventing problems.
- Notice and reward desirable behavior, and give him lots of attention when he is being good.
- Train ethically. Use humane methods and equipment that do not frighten or hurt your dog.
- When you are angry, walk away and plan a positive strategy.
- Keep practice sessions short and sweet. Five to ten minutes, three to five times a day is best.

when the punisher isn't around and the coast is clear, the same behavior he was punished for—such as raiding a trash can—might bring a self-delivered, very tasty result. The punished dog hasn't learned not to misbehave; he has learned to not get caught.

Does punishment ever have a place in dog training? Many people will heartily insist it does not. But dog owners often get frustrated as they try to stick to the path of all-positive reinforcement. It sure sounds great, but is it realistic, or even natural, to *never* say "no" to your dog?

A wild dog's life is not *all* positive. Hunger and thirst are both examples of negative reinforcement; the resulting discomfort motivates the wild dog to seek food and water. He encounters natural aversives such as pesky insects; mats in his coat; cold days; rainy days; sweltering hot days; and occasional run-ins with thorns, brambles, skunks, bees, and other nastiness. These all affect his behavior, as he tries to avoid the bad stuff whenever possible. The wild dog also occasionally encounters social punishers from others in his group when he gets too pushy. Starting with a growl or a snap from Mom, and later some mild and ritualized discipline from other members of his four-legged family, he learns to modify behaviors that elicit grouchy responses.

Our pet dogs don't naturally experience all positive results either, because they learn from their surroundings and from social experiences with other dogs. Watch a group of pet dogs playing together and you'll see a very old educational system still being used. As they wrestle and attempt to assert themselves, you'll notice many mouth-on-neck moments. Their playful biting is inhibited, with no intention to cause harm, but their message is clear: "Say uncle or this could hurt more!"

Observing that punishment does occur in nature, some people may feel compelled to try to be like the big wolf with their pet dogs. Becoming aggressive or heavy-handed with your pet will backfire! Your dog will not be impressed, nor will he want to follow you. Punishment causes dogs to change their behavior to avoid or escape discomfort and threats. Threatened dogs will either become very passive and offer submissive, appeasing postures, attempt to flee, or rise to the occasion and fight back. When people personally punish their dogs in an angry manner, one of these three defensive mechanisms will be triggered. Which one depends on a dog's genetic temperament as well as his past social experiences. Since we don't want to make our pets feel the need to avoid or escape us, personal punishment has no place in our training.

Remote Consequences

Sometimes, however, all-positive reinforcement is just not enough. That's because not all reinforcement comes from us. An inappropriate behavior can be self-reinforcing—just doing it makes the dog feel better in some way, whether you are there to say "good boy!" or not. Some examples are eating garbage, pulling the stuffing out of your sofa, barking at passersby, or urinating on the floor.

Although you don't want to personally punish your dog, the occasional deterrent may be called for to help derail these kinds of self-rewarding misbehaviors. In these cases, mild forms of impersonal or remote punishment can be used as part of a correction. The goal isn't to make your dog feel bad or to "know he has done wrong," but to help redirect him to alternate behaviors that are more acceptable to you.

The Problems with Personal Punishment

- Personally punished dogs are not taught appropriate behaviors.
- Personally punished dogs only stop misbehaving when they are caught or interrupted, but they don't learn not to misbehave when they are alone.
- Personally punished dogs become shy, fearful, and distrusting.
- Personally punished dogs may become defensively aggressive.
- Personally punished dogs become suppressed and inhibited.
- Personally punished dogs become stressed, triggering stress-reducing behaviors that their owners interpret as acts of spite, triggering even more punishment.
- Personally punished dogs have stressed owners.
- Personally punished dogs may begin to repeat behaviors they have been taught will result in negative, but predictable, attention.
- Personally punished dogs are more likely to be given away than are positively trained dogs.

You do this by pairing a slightly startling, totally impersonal sound with an equally impersonal and *very mild* remote consequence. The impersonal sound might be a single shake of an empty plastic pop bottle with pennies in it, held out of your dog's sight. Or you could use a vocal expression such as "eh!" delivered with you looking *away* from your misbehaving dog.

Pair your chosen sound—the penny bottle or "eh!"—with either a slight tug on his collar or a sneaky spritz on the rump from a water bottle. Do this right *as* he touches something he should not; bad timing will confuse your dog and undermine your training success.

To keep things under your control and make sure you get the timing right, it's best to do this as a setup. "Accidentally" drop a shoe on the floor, and then help your dog learn some things are best avoided. As he sniffs the shoe say "eh!" without looking at him and give a *slight* tug against his collar. This sound will quickly become meaningful as a correction all by itself—sometimes after just one setup—making the tug correction obsolete. The tug lets your dog see that you were right; going for that shoe *was* a bad idea! Your wise dog will be more likely to heed your warning next time, and probably move closer to you where it's safe. Be a good friend and pick up the nasty shoe. He'll be relieved and you'll look heroic. Later, when he's home alone and encounters a stray shoe, he'll want to give it a wide berth.

Your negative marking sound will come in handy in the future, when your dog begins to venture down the wrong behavioral path. The goal is not to announce your disapproval or to threaten your dog. You are not telling him to stop or showing how *you* feel about his behavior. You are sounding a warning to a friend who's venturing off toward danger—"I wouldn't if I were you!" Suddenly, there is an abrupt, rather startling, noise! Now is the moment to redirect him and help him earn positive reinforcement. That interrupted behavior will become something he wants to avoid in the future, but he won't want to avoid you.

Practical Commands for Family Pets

Before you begin training your dog, let's look at some equipment you'll want to have on hand:

- **A buckle collar** is fine for most dogs. If your dog pulls *very* hard, try a head collar, a device similar to a horse halter that helps reduce pulling by turning the dog's head. *Do not* use a choke chain (sometimes called a training collar), because they cause physical harm even when used correctly.
- **Six-foot training leash and twenty-six–foot retractable leash.**
- **A few empty plastic soda bottles with about twenty pennies in each one.** This will be used to impersonally interrupt misbehaviors before redirecting dogs to more positive activities.
- **A favorite squeaky toy,** to motivate, attract attention, and reward your dog during training.

Lure your dog to take just a few steps with you on the leash by being inviting and enthusiastic. Make sure you reward him for his efforts.

Baby Steps

Allow your young pup to drag a short, lightweight leash attached to a buckle collar for a few *supervised* moments, several times each day. At first the leash may annoy him and he may jump around a bit trying to get away from it. Distract him with your squeaky toy or a bit of his kibble and he'll quickly get used to his new "tail."

Begin walking him on the leash by holding the end and following him. As he adapts, you can begin to assert gentle direct pressure to teach him to follow you. Don't jerk or yank, or he will become afraid to walk when the leash is on. If he becomes hesitant, squat down facing him and let him figure out that by moving toward you he is safe and secure. If he remains confused or frightened and doesn't come to you, go to him and help him understand that you provide safe harbor while he's on the leash. Then back away a few steps and try again to lure him to you. As he learns that you are the "home base," he'll want to follow when you walk a few steps, waiting for you to stop, squat down, and make him feel great.

So Attached to You!

The next step in training your dog—and this is a very important one—is to begin spending at least an hour or more each day with him on a four- to six-foot leash, held by or tethered to you. This training will increase his attachment to you—literally!—as you sit quietly or walk about, tending to your household business. When you are quiet, he'll learn it is time to settle; when you are active, he'll learn to move with you. Tethering also keeps him out of trouble when you are busy but still want his company. It is a great alternative to confining a dog, and can be used instead of crating any time you're home and need to slow him down a bit.

Rotating your dog from supervised freedom to tethered time to some quiet time in the crate or his gated area gives him a diverse and balanced day while he is learning. Two confined or tethered hours is the most you should require of your dog in one stretch, before changing to some supervised freedom, play, or a walk.

The dog in training may, at times, be stressed by all of the changes he is dealing with. Provide a stress outlet, such as a toy to chew on, when he is confined or tethered. He will settle into his quiet time more quickly and completely. Always be sure to provide several rounds of daily play and free time (in a fenced area or on your retractable leash) in addition to plenty of chewing materials.

Tethering your dog is a great way to keep him calm and under control, but still with you.

Dog Talk

Dogs don't speak in words, but they do have a language—body language. They use postures, vocalizations, movements, facial gestures, odors, and touch—usually with their mouths—to communicate what they are feeling and thinking.

We also "speak" using body language. We have quite an array of postures, movements, and facial gestures that accompany our touch and language as we attempt to communicate with our pets. And our dogs can quickly figure us out!

Alone, without associations, words are just noises. But, because we pair them with meaningful body language, our dogs make the connection. Dogs can really learn to understand much of what we *say*, if what we *do* at the same time is consistent.

The Positive Marker

Start your dog's education with one of the best tricks in dog training: Pair various positive reinforcers—food, a toy, touch—with a sound such as a click on a clicker (which you can get at the pet supply store) or a spoken word like "good!" or "yes!" This will enable you to later "mark" your dog's desirable behaviors.

It seems too easy: Just say "yes!" and give the dog his toy. (Or use whatever sound and reward you have chosen.) Later, when you make your marking sound right at the instant your dog does the right thing, he will know you are going to be giving him something good for that particular action. And he'll be eager to repeat the behavior to hear you mark it again!

Next, you must teach your dog to understand the meaning of cues you'll be using to ask him to perform specific behaviors. This is easy, too. Does he already do things you might like him to do on command? Of course! He lies down, he sits, he picks things up, he drops them again, he comes to you. All of the behaviors you'd like to control are already part of your dog's natural repertoire. The trick is getting him to offer those behaviors when you ask for them. And that means you have to teach him to associate a particular behavior on his part with a particular behavior on your part.

Sit Happens

Teach your dog an important new rule: From now on, he is only touched and petted when he is either sitting or lying down. You won't need to ask him to sit; in fact, you should not. Just keeping him tethered near you so there isn't much to do but stand, be ignored, or settle, and wait until sit happens.

He may pester you a bit, but be stoic and unresponsive. Starting now, when *you* are sitting down, a sitting dog is the only one you see and pay attention to. He will eventually sit, and as he does, attach the word "sit"—but don't be too excited or he'll jump right back up. Now mark with your positive sound that promises something good, then reward him with a slow, quiet, settling pet.

Training requires consistent reinforcement. Ask others to also wait until your dog is sitting and calm to touch him, and he will associate being petted with being relaxed. Be sure you train your dog to associate everyone's touch with quiet bonding.

Reinforcing "Sit" as a Command

Since your dog now understands one concept of working for a living—sit to earn petting—you can begin to shape and reinforce his desire to sit. Hold toys, treats, his bowl of food, and turn into a statue. But don't prompt him to sit! Instead, remain frozen and unavailable, looking somewhere out into space, over his head. He will put on a bit of a show, trying to get a response from you, and may offer various behaviors, but only one will push your button—sitting. Wait for him to offer the "right" behavior, and when he does, you unfreeze. Say "sit," then mark with an excited "good!" and give him the toy or treat with a release command—"OK!"

When you notice spontaneous sits occurring, be sure to take advantage of those free opportunities to make your command sequence meaningful and positive. Say "sit" as you observe sit happen—then mark with "good!" and praise, pet, or reward the dog. Soon, every time you look at your dog he'll be sitting and looking right back at you!

Now, after thirty days of purely positive practice, it's time to give him a test. When he is just walking around doing his own thing, suddenly ask him to sit. He'll probably do it right away. If he doesn't, do *not* repeat your command, or you'll just undermine its meaning ("sit" means sit *now;* the command is not "sit, sit, sit, sit"). Instead, get something he likes and let him know you have it. Wait for him to offer the sit—he will—then say "sit!" and complete your marking and rewarding sequence.

OK

"OK" will probably rate as one of your dog's favorite words. It's like the word "recess" to schoolchildren. It is the word used to release your dog from a command. You can introduce "OK" during your "sit" practice. When he gets up from a sit, say "OK" to tell him the sitting is finished. Soon that sound will mean "freedom."

Make it even more meaningful and positive. Whenever he spontaneously bounds away, say "OK!" Squeak a toy, and when he notices and shows interest, toss it for him.

Down

I've mentioned that you should only pet your dog when he is either sitting or lying down. Now, using the approach I've just introduced for "sit," teach your dog to lie down. You will be a statue, and hold something he would like to get but that you'll only release to a dog who is lying down. It helps to lower the desired item to the floor in front of him, still not speaking and not letting him have it until he offers you the new behavior you are seeking.

Lower your dog's reward to the floor to help him figure out what behavior will earn him his reward.

He may offer a sit and then wait expectantly, but you must make him keep searching for the new trick that triggers your generosity. Allow your dog to experiment and find the right answer, even if he has to search around for it first. When he lands on "down" and learns it is another behavior that works, he'll offer it more quickly the next time.

Don't say "down" until he lies down, to tightly associate your prompt with the correct behavior. To say "down, down, down" as he is sitting, looking at you, or pawing at the toy would make "down" mean those behaviors instead! Whichever behavior he offers, a training opportunity has been created. Once you've attached and shaped both sitting and lying down, you can ask for both behaviors with your verbal prompts, "sit" or "down." Be sure to only reinforce the "correct" reply!

Stay

"Stay" can easily be taught as an extension of what you've already been practicing. To teach "stay," you follow the entire sequence for reinforcing a "sit" or "down," except you wait a bit longer before you give the release word, "OK!" Wait a second or two longer during each practice before saying "OK!" and releasing your dog to the positive reinforcer (toy, treat, or one of life's other rewards).

You can step on the leash to help your dog understand the down-stay, but only do this when he is already lying down. You don't want to hurt him!

If he gets up before you've said "OK," you have two choices: pretend the release was your idea and quickly interject "OK!" as he breaks; or, if he is more experienced and practiced, mark the behavior with your correction sound— "eh!"— and then gently put him back on the spot, wait for him to lie down, and begin again. Be sure the next three practices are a success. Ask him to wait for just a second, and release him before he can be wrong. You need to keep your dog feeling like more of a success than a failure as you begin to test his training in increasingly more distracting and difficult situations.

As he gets the hang of it—he stays until you say "OK"— you can gradually push for longer times—up to a minute on a sit-stay, and up to three minutes on a down-stay. You can also gradually add distractions and work in new environments. To add a minor self-correction for the down-stay, stand on the dog's leash after he lies down, allowing about three inches of slack. If tries to get up before you've said "OK," he'll discover it doesn't work.

Do not step on the leash to make your dog lie down! This could badly hurt his neck, and will destroy his trust in you. Remember, we are teaching our dogs to make the best choices, not inflicting our answers upon them!

Come

Rather than think of "come" as an action—"come to me"—think of it as a place—"the dog is sitting in front of me, facing me." Since your dog by now really likes sitting to earn your touch and other positive reinforcement, he's likely to sometimes sit directly in front of you, facing you, all on his own. When this happens, give it a specific name: "come."

Now follow the rest of the training steps you have learned to make him like doing it and reinforce the behavior by practicing it any chance you get. Anything your dog wants and likes could be earned as a result of his first offering the sit-in-front known as "come."

You can help guide him into the right location. Use your hands as "landing gear" and pat the insides of your legs at his nose level. Do this while backing up a bit, to help him maneuver to the straight-in-front, facing-you position. Don't say the

Pat the insides of your legs to show your dog exactly where you like him to sit when you say "come."

word "come" while he's maneuvering, because he hasn't! You are trying to make "come" the end result, not the work in progress.

You can also help your dog by marking his movement in the right direction: Use your positive sound or word to promise he is getting warm. When he finally sits facing you, enthusiastically say "come," mark again with your positive word, and release him with an enthusiastic "OK!" Make it so worth his while, with lots of play and praise, that he can't wait for you to ask him to come again!

Building a Better Recall

Practice, practice, practice. Now, practice some more. Teach your dog that all good things in life hinge upon him first sitting in front of you in a behavior named "come." When you think he really has got it, test him by asking him to "come" as you gradually add distractions and change locations. Expect setbacks as you make these changes and practice accordingly. Lower your expectations and make his task easier so he is able to get it right. Use those distractions as rewards, when they are appropriate. For example, let him check out the interesting leaf that blew by as a reward for first coming to you and ignoring it.

Add distance and call your dog to come while he is on his retractable leash. If he refuses and sits looking at you blankly, *do not* jerk, tug, "pop," or reel him in. Do nothing! It is his move; wait to see what behavior he offers. He'll either begin to approach (mark the behavior with an excited "good!"), sit and do nothing (just keep waiting), or he'll try to move in some direction other than toward you. If he tries to leave, use your correction marker—"eh!"— and bring him to a stop by letting him walk to the end of the leash, *not* by jerking him. Now walk to him in a neutral manner, and don't jerk or show any disapproval. Gently bring him back to the spot where he was when you called him, then back away and face him, still waiting and not reissuing your command. Let him keep examining his options until he finds the one that works—yours!

If you have practiced everything I've suggested so far and given your dog a chance to really learn what "come" means, he is well aware of what you want and is quite intelligently weighing all his options. The only way he'll know your way is the one that works is to be allowed to examine his other choices and discover that they *don't* work.

Sooner or later every dog tests his training. Don't be offended or angry when your dog tests you. No matter how positive you've made it, he won't always want to do everything you ask, every time. When he explores the "what happens if I don't" scenario, your training is being strengthened. He will discover through his own process of trial and error that the best—and only—way out of a command he really doesn't feel compelled to obey is to obey it.

Let's Go

Many pet owners wonder if they can retain control while walking their dogs and still allow at least some running in front, sniffing, and playing. You might worry that allowing your dog occasional freedom could result in him expecting it all the time, leading to a testy, leash-straining walk. It's possible for both parties on the leash to have an enjoyable experience by implementing and reinforcing well-thought-out training techniques.

Begin by making word associations you'll use on your walks. Give the dog some slack on the leash, and as he starts to walk away from you say "OK" and begin to follow him.

Do not let him drag you; set the pace even when he is being given a turn at being the leader. Whenever he starts to pull, just come to a standstill and refuse to move (or refuse to allow him to continue forward) until there is slack in the leash. Do this correction without saying anything at all. When he isn't pulling, you may decide to just stand still and let him sniff about within the range the slack leash allows, or you may even mosey along following him. After a few minutes of "recess," it is time to work. Say something like "that's it" or "time's up," close the distance between you and your dog, and touch him.

Next say "let's go" (or whatever command you want to use to mean "follow me as we walk"). Turn and walk off, and, if he follows, mark his behavior with "good!" Then stop,

Give your dog slack on his leash as you walk and let him make the decision to walk with you.

When your dog catches up with you, make sure you let him know what a great dog he is!

Intersperse periods of attentive walking, where your dog is on a shorter leash, with periods on a slack leash, where he is allowed to look and sniff around.

squat down, and let him catch you. Make him glad he did! Start again, and do a few transitions as he gets the hang of your follow-the-leader game, speeding up, slowing down, and trying to make it fun. When you stop, he gets to catch up and receive some deserved positive reinforcement. Don't forget that's the reason he is following you, so be sure to make it worth his while!

Require him to remain attentive to you. Do not allow sniffing, playing, eliminating, or pulling during your time as leader on a walk. If he seems to get distracted—which, by the way, is the main reason dogs walk poorly with their people— change direction or pace without saying a word. Just help him realize "oops, I lost track of my human." Do not jerk his neck and say "heel"—this will make the word "heel" mean pain in the neck and will not encourage him to cooperate with you. Don't repeat "let's go," either. He needs to figure out that it is his job to keep track of and follow you if he wants to earn the positive benefits you provide.

The best reward you can give a dog for performing an attentive, controlled walk is a few minutes of walking without all of the controls. Of course, he must remain on a leash even during the "recess" parts of the walk, but allowing him to discriminate between attentive following—"let's go"—and having a few moments of relaxation—"OK"—will increase his willingness to work.

Training for Attention

Your dog pretty much has a one-track mind. Once he is focused on something, everything else is excluded. This can be great, for instance, when he's focusing on you! But it can also be dangerous if, for example, his attention is riveted on the bunny he is chasing and he does not hear you call—that is, not unless he has been trained to pay attention when you say his name.

When you say your dog's name, you'll want him to make eye contact with you. Begin teaching this by making yourself so intriguing that he can't help but look.

When you call your dog's name, you will again be seeking a specific response—eye contact. The best way to teach this is to trigger his alerting response by making a noise with your mouth, such as whistling or a kissing sound, and then immediately doing something he'll find very intriguing.

You can play a treasure hunt game to help teach him to regard his name as a request for attention. As a bonus, you can reinforce the rest of his new vocabulary at the same time.

Treasure Hunt

Make a kissing sound, then jump up and find a dog toy or dramatically raid the fridge and rather noisily eat a piece of cheese. After doing this twice, make a kissing sound and then look at your dog.

Of course he is looking at you! He is waiting to see if that sound—the kissing sound—means you're going to go hunting again. After all, you're so good at it! Because he is looking, say his name, mark with "good," then go hunting and find his toy. Release it to him with an "OK." At any point if he follows you, attach your "let's go!" command; if he leaves you, give permission with "OK."

Using this approach, he cannot be wrong—any behavior your dog offers can be named. You can add things like "take it" when he picks up a toy, and "thank you" when he happens to drop one. Many opportunities to make your new vocabulary meaningful and positive can be found within this simple training game.

Problems to watch out for when teaching the treasure hunt:

- You really do not want your dog to come to you when you call his name (later, when you try to engage his attention to ask him to stay, he'll already be on his way toward you). You just want him to look at you.
- Saying "watch me, watch me" doesn't teach your dog to *offer* his attention. It just makes you a background noise.
- Don't lure your dog's attention with the reward. Get his attention and then reward him for looking. Try holding a toy in one hand with your arm stretched out to your side. Wait until he looks at you rather than the toy. Now say his name, then mark with "good!" and release the toy. As he goes for it, say "OK."

To get your dog's attention, try holding his toy with your arm out to your side. Wait until he looks at you, then mark the moment and give him the toy.

Teaching Cooperation

Never punish your dog for failing to obey you or try to punish him into compliance. Bribing, repeating yourself, and doing a behavior for him all avoid the real issue of dog training—his will. He must be helped to be willing, not made to achieve tasks. Good dog training helps your dog want to obey. He learns that he can gain what he values most through cooperation and compliance, and can't gain those things any other way.

Your dog is learning to *earn,* rather than expect, the good things in life. And you've become much more important to him than you were before. Because you are allowing him to experiment and learn, he doesn't have to be forced, manipulated, or bribed. When he wants something, he can gain it by cooperating with you. One of those "somethings"—and a great reward you shouldn't underestimate—is your positive attention, paid to him with love and sincere approval!

Chapter 10

Housetraining Your Golden Retriever

Excerpted from Housetraining: An Owner's Guide to a Happy Healthy Pet, 1st Edition, *by September Morn*

By the time puppies are about 3 weeks old, they start to follow their mother around. When they are a few steps away from their clean sleeping area, the mama dog stops. The pups try to nurse, but mom won't allow it. The pups mill around in frustration, then nature calls and they all urinate and defecate here, away from their bed. The mother dog returns to the nest, with her brood waddling behind her. Their first housetraining lesson has been a success.

The next one to housetrain puppies should be their breeder. The breeder watches as the puppies eliminate, then deftly removes the soiled papers and replaces them with clean papers before the pups can traipse back through their messes. He has wisely arranged the puppies' space so their bed, food, and drinking water are as far away from the elimination area as possible. This way, when the pups follow their mama, they will move away from their sleeping and eating area before eliminating. This habit will help the pups be easily housetrained.

Your Housetraining Shopping List

While your puppy's mother and breeder are getting her started on good housetraining habits, you'll need to do some shopping. If you have all the essentials in place before your dog arrives, it will be easier to help her learn the rules from day one.

Newspaper: The younger your puppy and larger her breed, the more newspapers you'll need. Newspaper is absorbent, abundant, cheap, and convenient.

Puddle Pads: If you prefer not to stockpile newspaper, a commercial alternative is puddle pads. These thick paper pads can be purchased under several trade names at pet supply stores. The pads have waterproof backing, so puppy urine doesn't seep through onto the floor. Their disadvantages are that they will cost you more than newspapers and that they contain plastics that are not biodegradable.

Poop Removal Tool: There are several types of poop removal tools available. Some are designed with a separate pan and rake, and others have the handles hinged like scissors. Some scoops need two hands for operation, while others are designed for one-handed use. Try out the different brands at your pet supply store. Put a handful of pebbles or dog kibble on the floor and then pick them up with each type of scoop to determine which works best for you.

Plastic Bags: When you take your dog outside your yard, you *must* pick up after her. Dog waste is unsightly, smelly, and can harbor disease. In many cities and towns, the law mandates dog owners clean up pet waste deposited on public ground. Picking up after your dog using a plastic bag scoop is simple. Just put your hand inside the bag, like a mitten, and then grab the droppings. Turn the bag inside out, tie the top, and that's that.

Crate: To housetrain a puppy, you will need some way to confine her when you're unable to supervise. A dog crate is a secure way to confine your dog for short periods during the day and to use as a comfortable bed at night. Crates come in wire mesh and in plastic. The wire ones are foldable to store flat in a smaller space. The plastic ones are more cozy, draft-free, and quiet, and are approved for airline travel.

Baby Gates: Since you shouldn't crate a dog for more than an hour or two at a time during the day, baby gates are a good way to limit your dog's freedom in the house. Be sure the baby gates you use are safe. The old-fashioned wooden, expanding lattice type has seriously injured a number of children by collapsing and trapping a leg, arm, or neck. That type of gate can hurt a puppy, too, so use the modern grid type gates instead. You'll need more than one baby gate if you have several doorways to close off.

Exercise Pen: Portable exercise pens are great when you have a young pup or a small dog. These metal or plastic pens are made of rectangular panels that are hinged together. The pens are freestanding, sturdy, foldable, and can be carried like a suitcase. You could set one up in your kitchen as the pup's daytime corral, and then take it outdoors to contain your pup while you garden or just sit and enjoy the day.

Enzymatic Cleaner: All dogs make housetraining mistakes. Accept this and be ready for it by buying an enzymatic cleaner made especially for pet accidents. Dogs like to eliminate where they have done it before, and lingering smells lead them to those spots. Ordinary household cleaners may remove all the odors you can smell, but only an enzymatic cleaner will remove everything your dog can smell.

The First Day

Housetraining is a matter of establishing good habits in your dog. That means you never want her to learn anything she will eventually have to unlearn. Start off housetraining on the right foot by teaching your dog that you prefer her to eliminate outside. Designate a potty area in your backyard (if you have one) or in the street in front of your home and take your dog to it as soon as you arrive home. Let her sniff a bit and, when she squats to go, give the action a name: "potty" or "do it" or anything else you won't be embarrassed to say in public. Eventually your dog will associate that word with the act and will eliminate on command. When she's finished, praise her with "good potty!"

That first day, take your puppy out to the potty area frequently. Although she may not eliminate every time, you are establishing a routine: You take her to her spot, ask her to eliminate, and praise her when she does.

Just before bedtime, take your dog to her potty area once more. Stand by and wait until she produces. Do not put your dog to bed for the night until she has eliminated. Be patient and calm. This is not the time to play with or excite your

Take your pup out frequently to her special potty spot and praise her when she goes.

dog. If she's too excited, a pup not only won't eliminate, she probably won't want to sleep either.

Most dogs, even young ones, will not soil their beds if they can avoid it. For this reason, a sleeping crate can be a tremendous help during housetraining. Being crated at night can help a dog develop the muscles that control elimination. So after your dog has emptied out, put her to bed in her crate.

A good place to put your dog's sleeping crate is near your own bed. Dogs are pack animals, so they feel safer sleeping with others in a common area. In your bedroom, the pup will be near you and you'll be close enough to hear when she wakes during the night and needs to eliminate.

Pups under 4 months old often are not able to hold their urine all night. If your puppy has settled down to sleep but awakens and fusses a few hours later, she probably needs to go out. For the best housetraining progress, take your pup to her elimination area whenever she needs to go, even in the wee hours of the morning.

Your pup may soil in her crate if you ignore her late night urgency. It's unfair to let this happen, and it sends the wrong message about your expectations for cleanliness. Resign yourself to this midnight outing and just get up and take the pup out. Your pup will outgrow this need soon and will learn in the process that she can count on you, and you'll wake happily each morning to a clean dog.

Don't Overuse the Crate

A crate serves well as a dog's overnight bed, but you should not leave the dog in her crate for more than an hour or two during the day. Throughout the day, she needs to play and exercise. She is likely to want to drink some water and will undoubtedly eliminate. Confining your dog all day will give her no option but to soil her crate. This is not just unpleasant for you and the dog, but it reinforces bad cleanliness habits. And crating a pup for the whole day is abusive. Don't do it.

The next morning, the very first order of business is to take your pup out to eliminate. Don't forget to take her to her special potty spot, ask her to eliminate, and then praise her when she does. After your pup empties out in the morning, give her breakfast, and then take her to her potty area again. After that, she shouldn't need to eliminate again right away, so you can allow her some free playtime. Keep an eye on the pup though, because when she pauses in play, she may need to go potty. Take her to the right spot, give the command, and praise if she produces.

Confine Your Pup

A pup or dog who has not finished housetraining should *never* be allowed the run of the house unattended. A new dog (especially a puppy) with unlimited access to your house will make her own choices about where to eliminate. Vigilance during your new dog's first few weeks in your home will pay big dividends. Every potty mistake delays housetraining progress; every success speeds it along.

Prevent problems by setting up a controlled environment for your new pet. A good place for a puppy corral is often the kitchen. Kitchens almost always have waterproof or easily cleaned floors, which is a distinct asset with leaky pups. A bathroom, laundry room, or enclosed porch could be used for a puppy corral, but the kitchen is generally the best location. Kitchens are a meeting place and a hub of activity for many families, and a puppy will learn better manners when she is socialized thoroughly with family, friends, and nice strangers.

The way you structure your pup's corral area is very important. Her bed, food, and water should be at the opposite end of the corral from the potty area. When you first get your pup, spread newspaper over the rest of the floor of her playpen corral. Lay the papers at least four pages thick and be sure to overlap the edges. As you note the pup's progress, you can remove the papers nearest the sleeping and eating corner. Gradually decrease the size of the papered area until only the end where you want the pup to eliminate is covered. If you will be training your dog to eliminate outside, place newspaper at the end of the corral that is closest to the door that leads outdoors. That way as she moves away from the clean area to

Your dog's crate is a great housetraining tool.

the papered area, the pup will also form the habit of heading toward the door to go out.

Maintain a scent marker for the pup's potty area by reserving a small soiled piece of paper when you clean up. Place this piece, with her scent of urine, under the top sheet of the clean papers you spread. This will cue your pup where to eliminate.

Most dog owners use a combination of indoor papers and outdoor elimination areas. When the pup is left by herself in the corral, she can potty on the ever-present newspaper. When you are available to take the pup outside, she can do her business in the outdoor spot. It is not difficult to switch a pup from indoor paper training to outdoor elimination. Owners of large pups often switch early, but potty papers are still useful if the pup spends time in her indoor corral while you're away. Use the papers as long as your pup needs them. If you come home and they haven't been soiled, you are ahead.

When setting up your pup's outdoor yard, put the lounging area as far away as possible from the potty area, just as with the indoor corral setup. People with large yards, for example, might leave a patch unmowed at the edge of the lawn to serve as the dog's elimination area. Other dog owners teach the dog to relieve herself in a designated corner of a deck or patio. For an apartment-dwelling city

Water

Make sure your dog has access to clean water at all times. Limiting the amount of water a dog drinks is not necessary for housetraining success and can be very dangerous. A dog needs water to digest food, to maintain a proper body temperature and proper blood volume, and to clean her system of toxins and wastes. A healthy dog will automatically drink the right amount. Do not restrict water intake. Controlling your dog's access to water is not the key to housetraining her; controlling her access to everything else in your home is.

dog, the outdoor potty area might be a tiny balcony or the curb. Each dog owner has somewhat different expectations for their dog. Teach your dog to eliminate in a spot that suits your environment and lifestyle.

Be sure to pick up droppings in your yard at least once a day. Dogs have a natural desire to stay far away from their own excrement, and if too many piles litter the ground, your dog won't want to walk through it and will start eliminating elsewhere. Leave just one small piece of feces in the potty area to remind your dog where the right spot is located.

To help a pup adapt to the change from indoors to outdoors, take one of her potty papers outside to the new elimination area. Let the pup stand on the paper when she goes potty outdoors. Each day for four days, reduce the size of the paper by half. By the fifth day, the pup, having used a smaller and smaller piece of paper to stand on, will probably just go to that spot and eliminate.

Designate some areas of the yard for eliminating and some for play, so your puppy won't be confused about what she is supposed to do when she is outside.

When you take your dog outside for a potty trip, don't play until after she's done. You don't want to distract her or confuse her about what this trip is for.

Take your pup to her outdoor potty place frequently throughout the day. A puppy can hold her urine for only about as many hours as her age in months, and will move her bowels as many times a day as she eats. So a 2-month-old pup will urinate about every two hours, while at 4 months she can manage about four hours between piddles. Pups vary somewhat in their rate of development, so this is not a hard and fast rule. It does, however, present a realistic idea of how long a pup can be left without access to a potty place. Past 4 months, her potty trips will be less frequent.

When you take the dog outdoors to her spot, keep her leashed so that she won't wander away. Stand quietly and let her sniff around in the designated area. If your pup starts to leave before she has eliminated, gently lead her back and remind her to go. If your pup sniffs at the spot, praise her calmly, say the command word, and just wait. If she produces, praise serenely, then give her time to sniff around a little more. She may not be finished, so give her time to go again before allowing her to play and explore her new home.

If you find yourself waiting more than five minutes for your dog to potty, take her back inside. Watch your pup carefully for twenty minutes, not giving her any opportunity to slip away to eliminate unnoticed. If you are too busy to watch the pup, put her in her crate. After twenty minutes, take her to the outdoor potty spot again and tell her what to do. If you're unsuccessful after five minutes, crate the dog again. Give her another chance to eliminate in fifteen or twenty minutes. Eventually, she will have to go.

Watch Your Pup

Be vigilant and don't let the pup make a mistake in the house. Each time you successfully anticipate elimination and take your pup to the potty spot, you'll move a step closer to your goal. Stay aware of your puppy's needs. If you ignore the pup, she will make mistakes and you'll be cleaning up more messes.

Keep a chart of your new dog's elimination behavior for the first three or four days. Jot down what times she eats, sleeps, and eliminates. After several days a pattern will emerge that can help you determine your pup's body rhythms. Most dogs tend to eliminate at fairly regular intervals. Once you know your new dog's natural rhythms, you'll be able to anticipate her needs and schedule appropriate potty outings.

Understanding the meanings of your dog's postures can also help you win the battle of the puddle. When your dog is getting ready to eliminate, she will display a specific set of postures. The sooner you can learn to read these signals, the cleaner your floor will stay.

A young puppy who feels the urge to eliminate may start to sniff the ground and walk in a circle. If the pup is very young, she may simply squat and go. All young puppies, male or female, squat to urinate. If you are housetraining a pup under 4 months of age, regardless of sex, watch for the beginnings of a squat as the signal to rush the pup to the potty area.

Housetraining is a huge task, but it doesn't go on forever. Be patient and eventually your puppy will be a reliable adult.

When a puppy is getting ready to defecate, she may run urgently back and forth or turn in a circle while sniffing or starting to squat. If defecation is imminent, the pup's anus may protrude or open slightly. When she starts to go, the pup will squat and hunch her back, her tail sticking straight out behind. There is no mistaking this posture; nothing else looks like this. If your pup takes this position, take her to her potty area. Hurry! You may have to carry her to get there in time.

A young puppy won't have much time between feeling the urge and actually eliminating, so you'll have to be quick to note her postural clues and intercept your pup in time. Pups from 3 to 6 months have a few seconds more between the urge and the act than younger ones do. The older your pup, the more time you'll have to get her to the potty area after she begins the posture signals that alert you to her need.

Accidents Happen

If you see your pup about to eliminate somewhere other than the designated area, interrupt her immediately. Say "wait, wait, wait!" or clap your hands loudly to startle her into stopping. Carry the pup, if she's still small enough, or take her collar and lead her to the correct area. Once your dog is in the potty area, give her the command to eliminate. Use a friendly voice for the command, then wait patiently for her to produce. The pup may be tense because you've just startled her and may have to relax a bit before she's able to eliminate. When she does her job, include the command word in the praise you give ("good potty").

The old-fashioned way of housetraining involved punishing a dog's mistakes even before she knew what she was supposed to do. Puppies were punished for breaking rules they didn't understand about functions they couldn't control. This was not fair. While your dog is new to housetraining, there is no need or excuse for punishing her mistakes. Your job is to take the dog to the potty area just before she needs to go, especially with pups under 3 months old. If you aren't watching your pup closely enough and she has an accident, don't punish the puppy for your failure to anticipate her needs. It's not the pup's fault; it's yours.

In any case, punishment is not an effective tool for housetraining most dogs. Many will react to punishment by hiding puddles and feces where you won't find them right away (like behind the couch or under the desk). This eventually may lead to punishment after the fact, which leads to more hiding, and so on.

Instead of punishing for mistakes, stay a step ahead of potty accidents by learning to anticipate your pup's needs. Accompany your dog to the designated

It's not fair to expect your baby puppy to be able to control herself the way an adult dog can.

potty area when she needs to go. Tell her what you want her to do and praise her when she goes. This will work wonders. Punishment won't be necessary if you are a good teacher.

What happens if you come upon a mess after the fact? Some trainers say a dog can't remember having eliminated, even a few moments after she has done so. This is not true. The fact is that urine and feces carry a dog's unique scent, which she (and every other dog) can instantly recognize. So, if you happen upon a potty mistake after the fact you can still use it to teach your dog.

But remember, no punishment! Spanking, hitting, shaking, or scaring a puppy for having a housetraining accident is confusing and counterproductive. Spend your energy instead on positive forms of teaching.

Take your pup and a paper towel to the mess. Point to the urine or feces and calmly tell your puppy, "no potty here." Then scoop or sop up the accident with the paper towel. Take the evidence and the pup to the approved potty area. Drop the mess on the ground and tell the dog, "good potty here," as if she had done the deed in the right place. If your pup sniffs at the evidence, praise her calmly. If the accident happened very recently your dog may not have to go yet, but wait with her a few minutes anyway. If she eliminates, praise her. Afterwards, go finish cleaning up the mess.

Soon the puppy will understand that there is a place where you are pleased about elimination and other places where you are not. Praising for elimination in the approved place will help your pup remember the rules.

Scheduling Basics

With a new puppy in the home, don't be surprised if your rising time is suddenly a little earlier than you've been accustomed to. Puppies have earned a reputation as very early risers. When your pup wakes you at the crack of dawn, you will have to get up and take her to her elimination spot. Be patient. When your dog is an adult, she may enjoy sleeping in as much as you do.

At the end of the chapter, you'll find a typical housetraining schedule for puppies aged 10 weeks to 6 months. (To find schedules for younger and older pups, and for adult dogs, visit this book's companion Web site.) It's fine to adjust the rising times when using this schedule, but you should not adjust the intervals between feedings and potty outings unless your pup's behavior justifies a change. Your puppy can only meet your expectations in housetraining if you help her learn the rules.

The schedule for puppies is devised with the assumption that someone will be home most of the time with the pup. That would be the best scenario, of course, but is not always possible. You may be able to ease the problems of a latchkey pup by having a neighbor or friend look in on the pup at noon and take her to eliminate. A better solution might be hiring a pet sitter to drop by midday. A professional pet sit-

ter will be knowledgeable about companion animals and can give your pup high-quality care and socialization. Some can even help train your pup in both potty manners and basic obedience. Ask your veterinarian and your dog-owning friends to recommend a good pet sitter.

If you must leave your pup alone during her early housetraining period, be sure to cover the entire floor of her corral with thick layers of overlapping newspaper. If you come home to messes in the puppy corral, just clean them up. Be patient—she's still a baby.

Use this schedule (and the ones on the companion Web site) as a basic plan to help prevent housetraining accidents. Meanwhile, use your own powers of observation to

Setting up a regular schedule will help make housetraining a lot more predictable. For example, puppies always need to go soon after they wake up.

discover how to best modify the basic schedule to fit your dog's unique needs. Each dog is an individual and will have her own rhythms, and each dog is reliable at a different age.

Schedule for Pups 10 Weeks to 6 Months

7:00 a.m.	Get up and take the puppy from her sleeping crate to her potty spot.
7:15	Clean up last night's messes, if any.
7:30	Food and fresh water.
7:45	Pick up the food bowl. Take the pup to her potty spot; wait and praise.
8:00	The pup plays around your feet while you have your breakfast.
9:00	Potty break (younger pups may not be able to wait this long).
9:15	Play and obedience practice.
10:00	Potty break.
10:15	The puppy is in her corral with safe toys to chew and play with.
11:30	Potty break (younger pups may not be able to wait this long).
11:45	Food and fresh water.
12:00 p.m.	Pick up the food bowl and take the pup to her potty spot.
12:15	The puppy is in her corral with safe toys to chew and play with.
1:00	Potty break (younger pups may not be able to wait this long).
1:15	Put the pup on a leash and take her around the house with you.
3:30	Potty break (younger pups may not be able to wait this long).
3:45	Put the pup in her corral with safe toys and chews for solitary play and/or a nap.
4:45	Potty break.

5:00	Food and fresh water.
5:15	Potty break.
5:30	The pup may play nearby (either leashed or in her corral) while you prepare your evening meal.
7:00	Potty break.
7:15	Leashed or closely watched, the pup may play and socialize with family and visitors.
9:15	Potty break (younger pups may not be able to wait this long).
10:45	Last chance to potty.
11:00	Put the pup to bed in her crate for the night.

Learning More About Your Golden Retriever

Some Good Books

About Golden Retrievers

Berger, Todd R., *Love of Goldens: The Ultimate Tribute to Golden Retrievers,* Voyageur Press, 2003.

Cairns, Julie, *The Golden Retriever: All That Glitters,* Howell Book House, 1998.

Davis, Tom, *Why Goldens Do That: A Collection of Curious Golden Retriever Behaviors,* Willow Creek Press, 2005.

Foss, Valerie, *The Ultimate Golden Retriever,* 2nd edition, Howell Book House, 2003.

About Health Care

Acker, Randy, DVM, and Jim Fergus, *Field Guide: Dog First Aid Emergency Care for the Hunting, Working, and Outdoor Dog,* Wilderness Adventures Press, 1994.

Eldredge, Debra, DVM, and Delbert Carlson, DVM, Liisa Carlson, DVM, James Giffin, MD, *Dog Owner's Home Veterinary Handbook,* 4th edition, Howell Book House, 2007.

Fogle, Bruce, DVM, *First Aid for Dogs: What to Do When Emergencies Happen,* Penguin, 1997.

Morgan, Diane, *The Living Well Guide for Senior Dogs,* TFH Publications, 2007.

Zink, M. Christine, DVM, PhD, *Dog Health & Nutrition For Dummies,* John Wiley and Sons, 2001.

About Training

Ammen, Amy, and Kitty Foth-Regner, *Hip Ideas for Hyper Dogs,* Howell Book House, 2007.

Barlow, Vic, *British Training for American Retrievers: Unleash Your Dog's Natural Talent,* Willow Creek Press, 2003.

Palika, Liz, *How to Train Your Golden Retriever,* TFH Publications, 1998.

Rutherford, Clarice, and David H. Neil, *How to Raise a Puppy You Can Live With,* 4th edition, Alpine Blue Ribbon Books, 2005.

Canine Activities

Arden, Darlene, *Unbelievably Good Deals and Great Adventures That You Absolutely Can't Get Unless You're a Dog,* McGraw-Hill, 2004.

Bonham, Margaret H., *The Simple Guide to Getting Active with Your Dog,* TFH Publications, 2002.

Owens Wright, Sue, *150 Activities for Bored Dogs: Surefire Ways to Keep Your Dog Active and Happy,* Adams Media, 2007.

Magazines

AKC Family Dog
AKC Gazette
American Kennel Club
260 Madison Ave.
New York, NY 10016
(212) 696-8200
www.akc.org

The Bark
2810 8th St.
Berkeley, CA 94710
(877) 227-5639
www.thebark.com

Dog Fancy
Dog World
P.O. Box 37186
Boone, IA 50037-0186
(800) 896-4939
www.dogfancy.com
www.dogworldmag.com

Dog Watch
P.O. Box 420235
Palm Coast, FL 32142-0235
(800) 829-5574
www.vet.cornell.edu/
publicresources/dog.htm

Gun Dog
P.O. Box 420235
Palm Coast, FL 32142-0235
(800) 274-6386
www.gundogmag.com

Clubs and Registries

Golden Retriever Club of America
Deborah Ascher, Membership Administrator
P.O. Box 69
Berthoud, CO 80513-0069
www.grca.org
This is the national club for the breed; its web site has a great deal of information, including upcoming shows and competitions. There are also many all-breed, individual breed, canine sport, and other special-interest dog clubs across the country. The registries listed below can help you find clubs in your area.

American Kennel Club
260 Madison Ave.
New York, NY 10016
(212) 696-8200
www.akc.org

Canadian Kennel Club
89 Skyway Ave., Suite 100
Etobicoke, Ontario
Canada M9W 6R4
(800) 250-8040 or (416) 675-5511
www.ckc.ca

United Kennel Club
100 E. Kilgore Rd.
Kalamazoo, MI 49001-5598
(269) 343-9020
www.ukcdogs.com

On the Internet

All About Goldens

Canadian Goldens
www.canadiangoldens.com/
Canadian Goldens offers a comprehensive Web site for Golden enthusiasts.

The Golden Retriever Club
www.thegoldenretrieverclub.co.uk
The Web site for the original Golden Retriever Club, started by Mrs. Charlesworth in 1913 in the United Kingdom. This site has lots of interesting information about British Goldens.

Golden Retriever Club of America National Rescue Committee
www.grca-nrc.org/
This is a great place to start if you are hoping to adopt a Golden Retriever; includes contact information for state rescue organizations, as well as helpful information specific to Golden adoptions.

The Golden Retriever WebRing
www.webring.com/hub?ring=goldenretr
The Golden Retriever WebRing provides fanciers with their own home pages and a forum to share and exchange information, as well as quick access to related Golden Retriever sites.

Canine Health

American Veterinary Medical Association
www.avma.org
The American Veterinary Medical Association Web site with a wealth of information for dog owners, from disaster preparedness to both common and rare diseases affecting canines. There is also information on choosing the right dog and dog-bite prevention.

Canine Health Information Center
www.caninehealthinfo.org
The Canine Health Information Center is a centralized canine health database jointly sponsored by the American Kennel Club Canine Health Foundation and the Orthopedic Foundation for Animals.

Dog Sports and Activities

American Society for the Prevention of Cruelty to Animals
www.aspca.org
Humane education and advocacy.

Bird Dog & Retriever News
www.bird-dog-news.com
A huge online and print hunting-dog magazine, with hundreds of archived articles.

Dog Friendly
www.dogfriendly.com
Information about traveling with dogs.

Dog Patch
www.dogpatch.org
Information on many different dog sports and activities, including herding, agility, and Frisbee.

Dog Play
www.dogplay.com
More about dog sports and activities, including hiking, backpacking, therapy-dog work, and much more.

Working Dogs
www.workingdogs.com
An Internet magazine for people who own or train working dogs of all kinds.

Working Retriever Central
www.working-retriever.com
All about buying working retrievers, training working retrievers, and much more.

Index